The Song Inside of Things

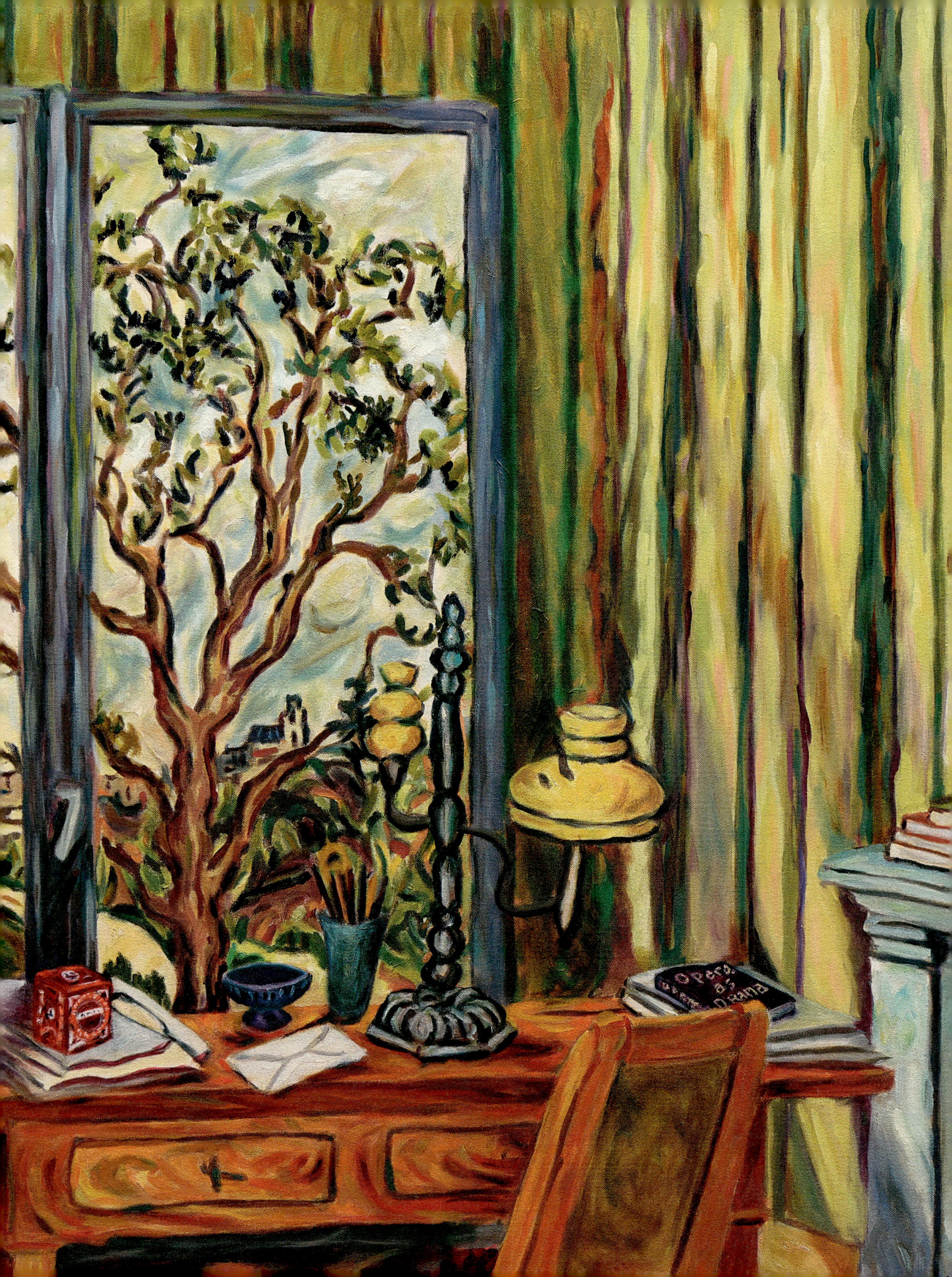

Helen Berggruen

The Song Inside of Things

HURTWOOD

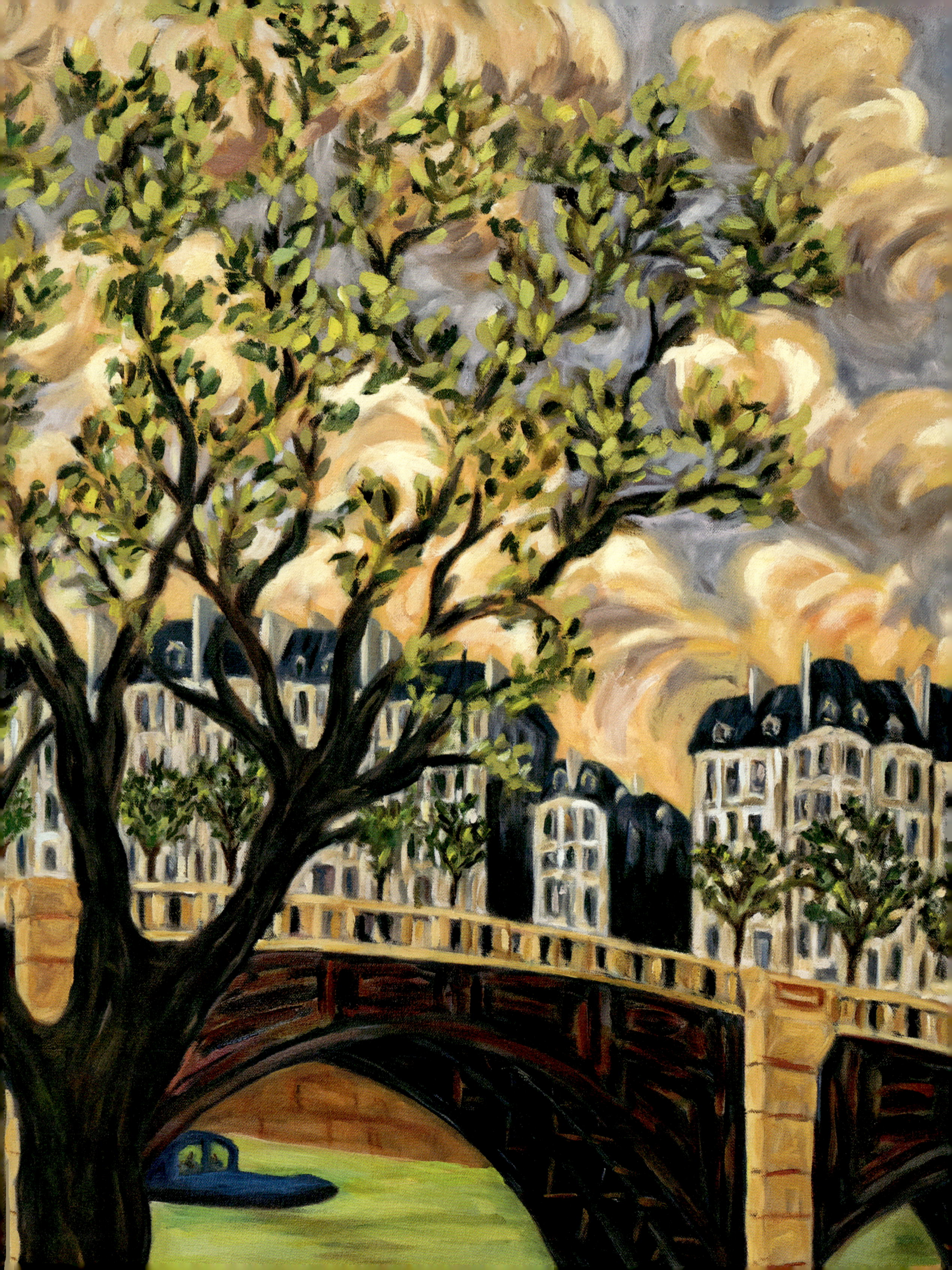

Contents

Previous page:
Interior with Matadors, 2018
(detail)
Oil on linen
121.9 × 101.6 cm
48 × 40 in

Pont de la Tournelle, 1995–2025
(detail)
Oil on linen
94 × 81.3 cm
37 × 32 in

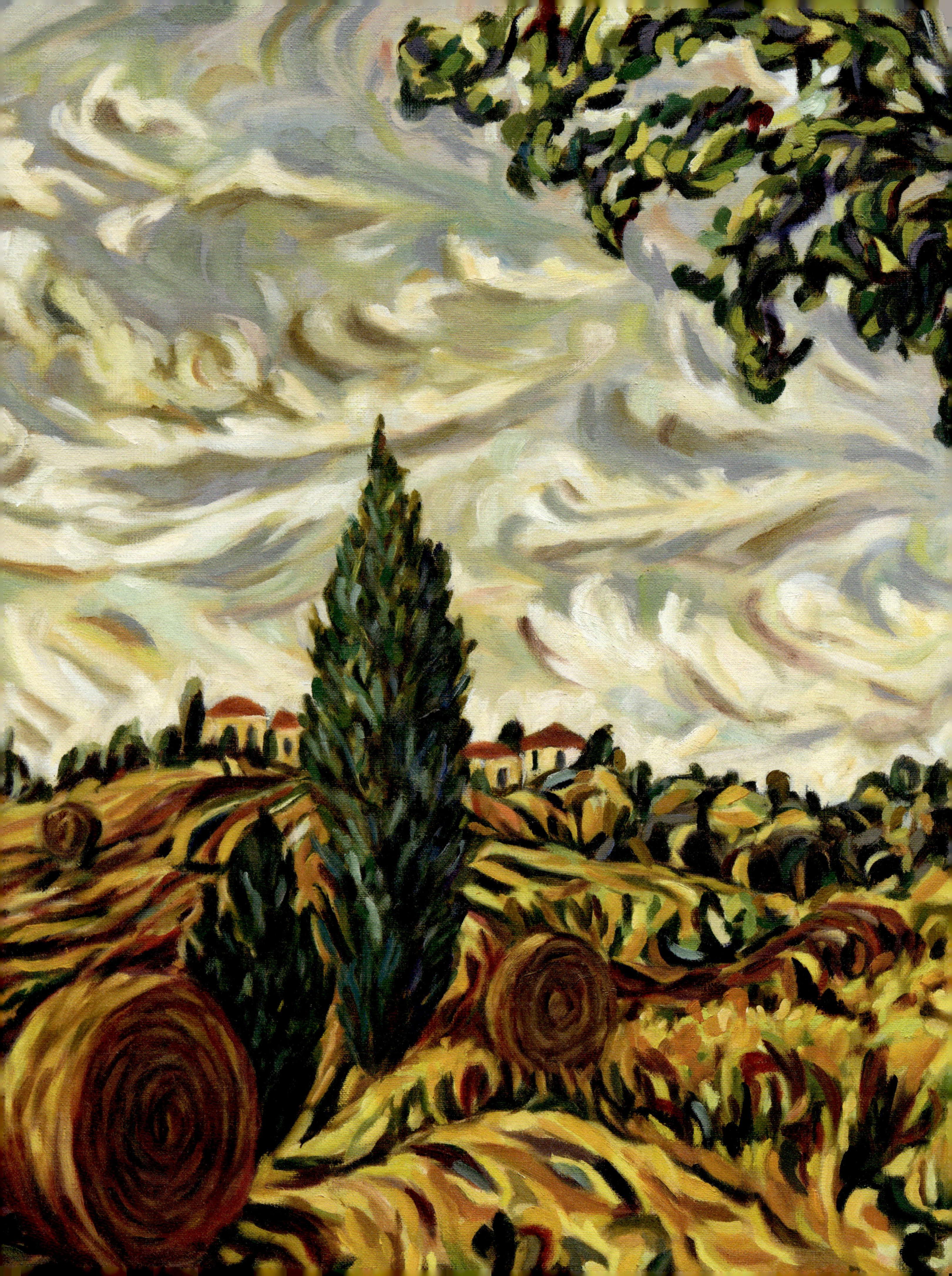

Foreword
Mary Kate Tankard

Helen Berggruen's paintings depict a theatrically charged reality. Her expressive, gestural practice animates landscapes, still lifes and interior scenes by affording each compositional detail its own energy. Mixed textures, robust patterns and a full-spectrum palette convey her generous illuminations. Berggruen's paintings portray the windows that emerge, however briefly and rarely, when a note, a song or the presence of a performer is so sublime, so arresting, so all-encompassing, that time and space have no choice but to defer.

Berggruen began her artistic career on the stage. The theatre was her first painterly language. As an undergraduate at Sarah Lawrence College, Berggruen took courses in the dance and theatre departments, and began acting in experimental theatre troupes with her peers. On weekends, she would take the train into New York City, where she found herself among the experimental visual art and theatre scene of the late sixties and early seventies. It was here that she encountered the avant-garde director, playwright and visual artist Robert Wilson and became a member of the Byrd Hoffman School of Byrds. Berggruen would later call this 'a time of complete inspiration'.

Wilson's productions were based on time, space and silence. Often plotless and without characters in a traditional sense, Wilson emphasised storytelling through absence, pushing the audience into trance-like states of observation and anticipation. He employed the body sculpturally. Dancers set like metronomes; a single motion such as an arm moving or an eyebrow being raised might be painstakingly suspended over five minutes. Stillness was tempo. Music was made architectural; image and sound were of equal importance.

Hay Rolls, Road to St. Martin, 2025
(detail)
Oil on linen
60.3 × 73 cm
23¾ × 28¾ in

When Berggruen decided to leave New York City and move to Napa Valley to dedicate herself full-time to painting, she wondered whether the energetic transference that occurred between audience and performer, which she had for so many years lived on stage, could be achieved on canvas. Whether, like a Wilson production, a painting could ask the viewer to *listen with their eyes*. She set out to create a body of work in which dissonance and tonal asymmetry could reach resolution, where gestures could be applied rhythmically, in time and tempo, to transform the mundane – the quotidian – into something enchanted.

Berggruen travelled all over Europe and the USA for the theatre, first as a performer during her time working with Wilson and later as a devotee of the opera singer Joyce DiDonato. During these travels Berggruen sketched *en plein air* and in museums. These pencil drawings sat tucked away in her sketchbooks for years before eventually becoming the subjects of her paintings. While Berggruen was interested in the stylistic principles of German Expressionist and post-Impressionist painters, her love of the opera – and specifically the effect of DiDonato's performances – inspired her to begin making sketches of Renaissance sculptures and eighteenth and nineteenth-century Romantic portraiture. In her correspondence with DiDonato, Berggruen wrote that the singer's voice held 'illumination, the power to transform, and the link to the sublime'.

While Berggruen's gestures evoke the stylistic innovations of van Gogh, her expressions reflect an artistic state that is playful, exuberant – joyful rather than tortured. Objects dance across a table's surface. Paintbrushes, scissors and stacks of books abound. Tractors and trucks move languidly over Parisian cobblestones and through agrarian and industrial landscapes. Berggruen's work hints at narratives full of adventure and travel. These paintings embody and advocate a belief in work that can occupy a space that is both serious and spirited – a glimpse into the grand opera that can be everyday life if only one might tune into the measures imbued within.

***Cattle Ranch Hand*, 2023**
(detail)
Oil on linen
55.9 × 71.1 cm
22 × 28 in

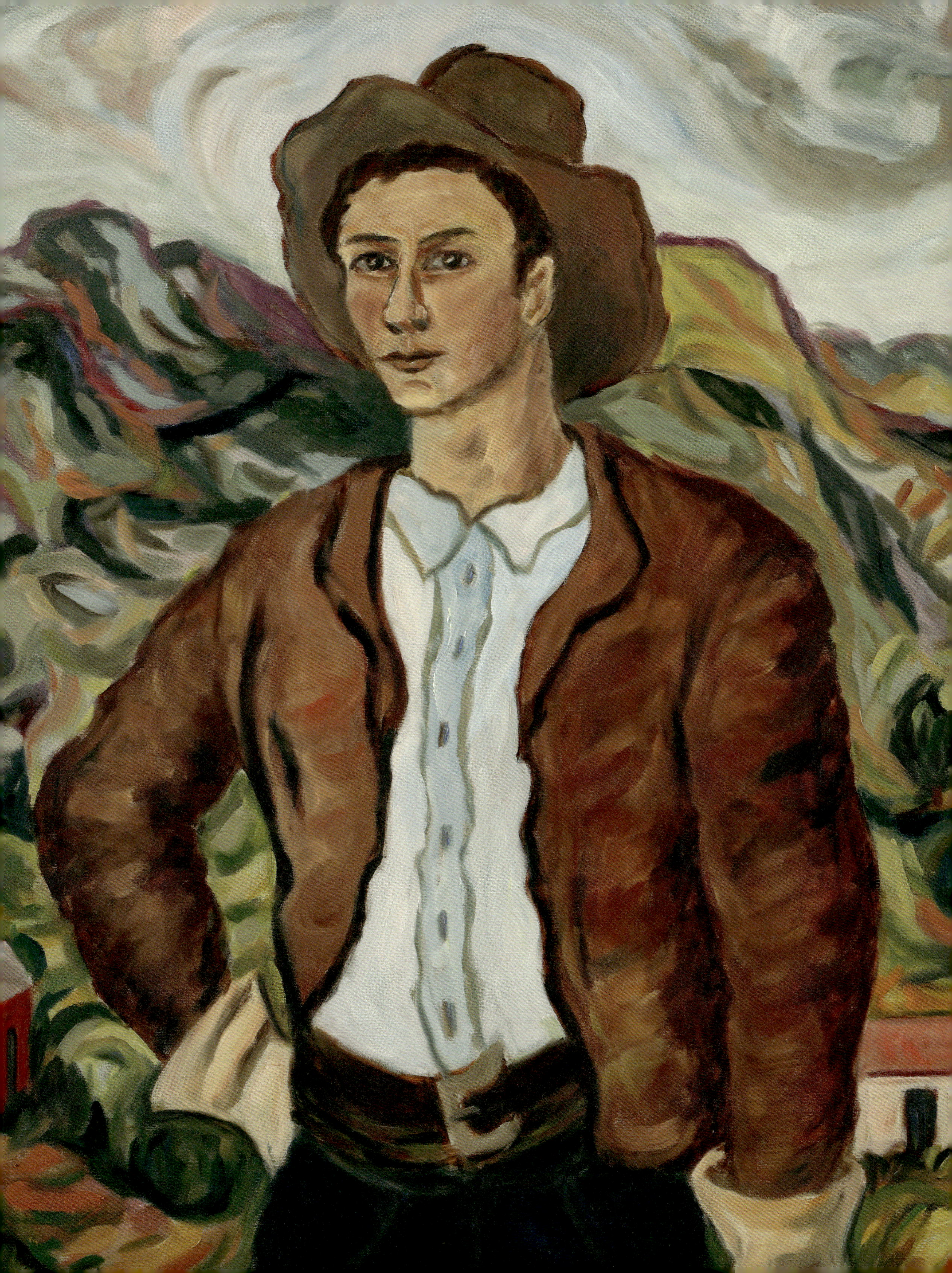

Everyday Enchantments
Craig Burnett

Helen Berggruen's landscapes and interiors look reassuringly familiar. Rooftops, rivers, views through windows, cement trucks, cups and quartered oranges animate her canvases, each thing fulfilling its destiny in a balanced domestic or political ecosystem. Beyond this air of familiarity, however, her paintings reveal a world where time is out of joint. A world haunted by the imagination. A passage of molten sky, a book balanced at the edge of a desk, a boat puttering on an emerald river, or a casually abandoned ladder – all these everyday details flicker with a restless vivacity, even a hint of sentience.

The windows in *Paris Cement Mixers* (2025) are like the avid eyes of a child, animating the scene before them. Three cement trucks (one just out of frame to the left), painted in vivid reds and yellows, occupy the middle ground of the painting, signing off after a day maintaining one of the world's most beautiful cities. Despite the absence of human figures, the scene hums with arrested busyness. A red, diamond-shaped bucket sways across flowing green leaves, while great slabs of timber, and a ladder, are arrayed at jaunty angles in the foreground, a reminder that Berggruen once trained and worked as a carpenter and construction worker. Even the sky, a restless gurgle of pastel blues and yellows, seems to be wondering what to do next. The clock on the church tower appears to read about five to six, suggesting the builders have just hit the road, leaving their job unfinished until the next day. All this beauty, planned and built hundreds of years ago, requires care and maintenance – an act of beauty in itself.

Paris Cement Mixers reveals a lot about Berggruen's artistic vision. The clock tower looms over the scene like the unappeasable eye of a god, emphasising how beholden we are to schedules and the passage of time. There are multiple registers of history, from the eighteenth- and nineteenth-century buildings to the cement mixers, which look

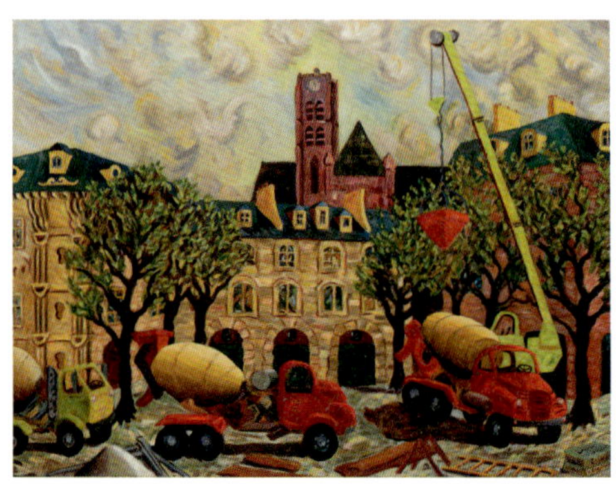

***Paris Cement Mixers*, 2025**
Oil on canvas
91.4 × 121.9 cm
36 × 48 in

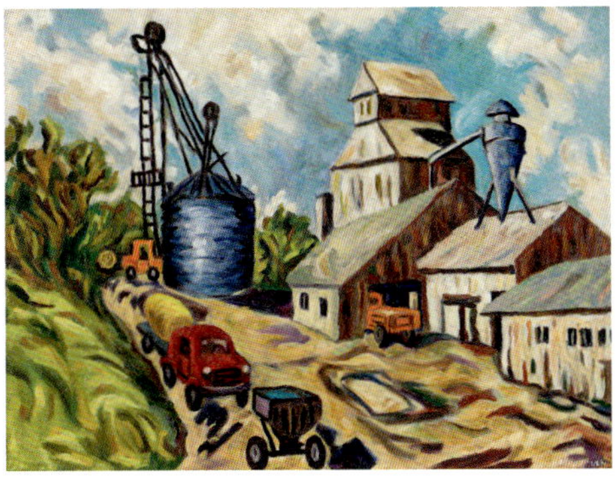

***Silos in Oxford, Iowa*, 2005–25**
Oil on linen
45.7 cm × 61 cm
18 × 24 in

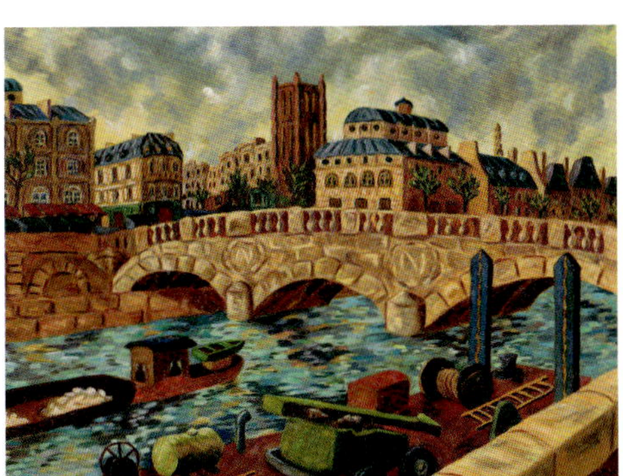

***Pont au Change*, 1995–2025**
Oil on canvas
80 × 105.4 cm
31½ × 41½ in

slightly anachronistic, as if they emerged from the 1950s. And there's the sense of maintenance itself, that buildings, cities, lives, everything needs to be looked after, kept alive against the ravages of time. There's also a mix of high and low, with a Parisian skyline that is synonymous with centuries of urban sophistication, while the workaday trucks are content and comfortable in this company, like humble doctors to the immortals, maintaining the health of the city. Time itself appears to be suspended like the bucket of cement, the day unfinished, the world taking a break, readying itself for the inevitability of another day. Crucially, there is also a feeling of aliveness everywhere, from the fleshy warmth of the architecture to the catchlight windows, the floridity of the sky and the shifting colours of the ground. Berggruen captures time at its most varied and complex – as lush and tactile as it is fugitive – and contains an infinite moment in a painting.

Farms might seem as old as time, and are synonymous with both backbreaking labour and civilisation: with agriculture came time for leisure, free time transmuted into forms of abstraction such as daydreaming and art. Berggruen's Iowan farm paintings differ from her normal method: she usually begins with a pencil drawing – and in some cases, a drawing will be set aside for decades – before transforming sketch into painting at her studio. Paintings of farms, by contrast, are made on site, and *en plein air.* In *Silos in Oxford, Iowa* (2005-25), there's a truck reminiscent of those in *Paris Cement Mixers,* a deep red and yellow pair of primary colours embedded amid a landscape of secondary hues such as green trees and grasses, two orange trucks, touches of purple on the ground. The silo in *Elkander Co-op* (2005–25), conjured with boldly palpable brushstrokes, shimmers like a river, at once beautiful and proud, while the whole composition, balanced by the dominant primary reds and blues, expresses a vibrant optimism. Berggruen depicts these farms as sites of essential goodness, places where human beings work with the unpredictable forces of nature to produce food for the community. Tapping into a tradition in American art, from Grant Wood to Thomas Hart Benton, even Walker Evans, Berggruen celebrates labour, recognising that farms revolve around the seasons, and honour our ties to the earth.

Culturally and geographically many miles away, Paris is one of Berggruen's most beloved subjects. A city renowned for its timeless elegance, she sees in its streets, gardens and bridges a vulnerable body, with layers and moving parts that require, not unlike a farm, endless care and maintenance. Compare the Paris painting *Pont au Change* (1995-2025) to *Silos in Oxford, Iowa.* A completely different setting, yet animated by a similar set of ideas and sentiments, emphasised by the formal structure and composition of both paintings. Rather than a pair of lovesick newlyweds or gawping tourists, a world of industry occupies the foreground of the painting. A mobile dock or barge hugs the wall along the Seine, filled with ladders, huge spools of rope, a fuel tank and other accoutrements of industry. Meanwhile, in the background, a small tug put-puts along, pulling a barge full of stones, its figurehead a small green rowing boat. The surface of the river is a shifting mosaic of blues and ochre reflections, while La Tour St Jacques rises from the horizon like a silo in Iowa. Further in the background we find trees and booksellers' kiosks, tight rows of windows under Mansard roofs, the city depicted in a way that makes Paris more snug and jumbled than usual, conveying a sense that all things are connected and dependent on each other, that the city itself is a living body, its labourers as essential as the rich who dwell within.

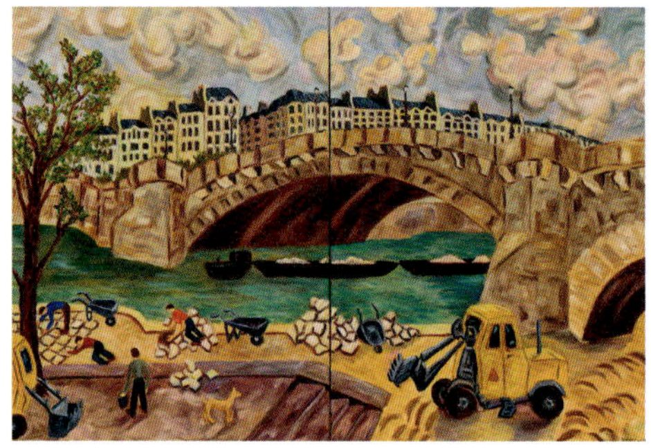

Stonework, Quai Conti **(diptych), 1994–2025**
Oil on linen
73 cm × 108 cm
28¾ × 42½ in

Across the Seine from the Louvre, between Pont Neuf and Pont des Arts, the Quai de Conti is an artery at the heart of Parisian history. Berggruen's diptych *Stonework, Quai Conti* (1994–2025) depicts a city in flux and repair, kept alive by masons and builders. The painting shares with *Pont au Change* a similar pictorial structure, with the arch of a bridge occupying the middle ground of the composition, Haussmann's acclaimed skyline in the background, and a world of workers and their tools in the foreground. As the masons ply their trade, highlighted by their primary red and blue T-shirts, the piles of stones echo the forms of the cumulus clouds, and a lone tree looks on approvingly while a yellow dog raises its head at the top of a purple staircase. Berggruen infuses the painting with energy and dynamism by composing with juxtaposed, interacting complementary colours, showing the influence of Maurice de Vlaminck and Fernand Léger. The painting also doffs its hat to Jean-François Millet's *The Gleaners* (1857): a nineteenth-century forebear who honoured labour with equal zeal, depicting workers as essential elements in the landscape, harmonised with nature. Although a painting such as *Stonework, Quai Conti* might begin in observation, Berggruen layers her paintings with allusions to art-historical figures to articulate a vision of the present that emphasises memory, care and maintenance. It's also worth pointing out the long gestation period of the painting: started and reworked from a drawing over a period of thirty years. As Paris needs a lot of attention over time, so do Berggruen's paintings.

A quality of *in medias res*, of narratives unfinished and unfolding, characterises the atmosphere in many of Berggruen's works. *Le Salon de Mme Basseraux* (2001–25) shares with *Paris Cement Mixers* the feeling of a day and its activities ended, if temporarily. The chairs are pushed back as if everyone attending was called away, and yet the room still seems to echo with lively conversation. On the table, a glass, a cup of coffee, a bowl of fruit, a few books – a conventional still life, everything ready to be taken up again within moments. The table looks almost

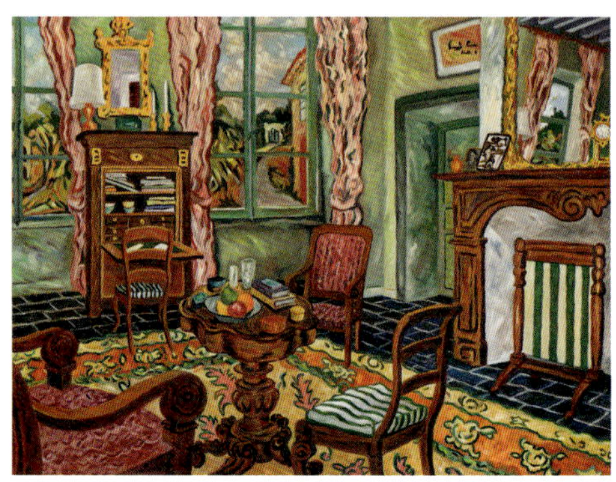

Le Salon de Mme Basseraux**, 2001–25**
Oil on linen
121.9 × 162.6 cm
48 × 64 in

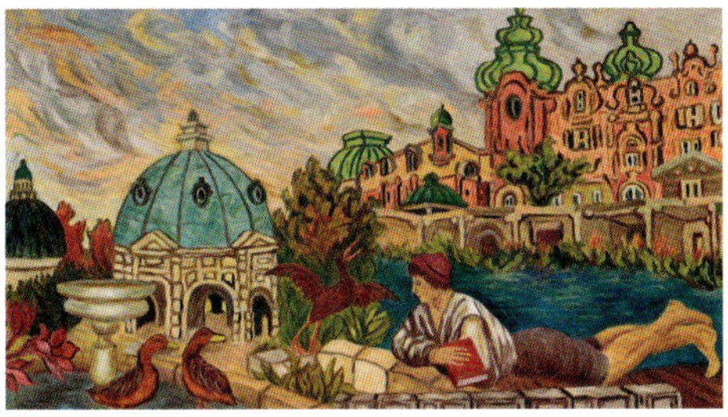

Song of the Water Rail, 2025
Oil on linen
61 × 111.8 cm
24 × 44 in

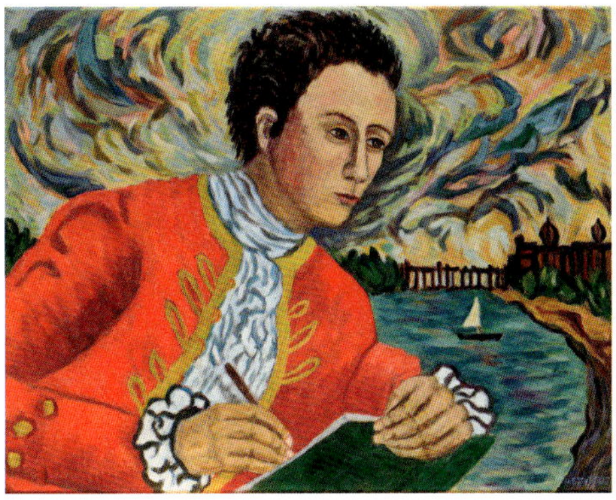

Appoggiatura, 2025
Oil on linen
55.9 × 71.1 cm
22 × 28 in

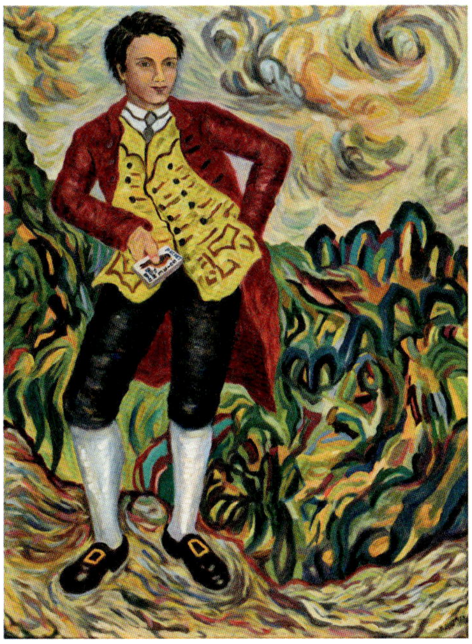

Pocket Guide to British Birds, 2025
Oil on linen
101.6 × 76.2 cm
40 × 30 in

molten, efflorescing at the centre of the room like a fountain. The depiction of light in the interior is a character in itself, with dashes of yellow and cream caressing the walls, while the curtains that frame the window writhe with visceral energy. The patch of clouds, as usual for Berggruen, tells its own story, of fidget and flow, of the evanescence of any day. Adding to the overall sense of a world as a multifaceted, shifting image is the presence of a few pictures in the room. There are two mirrors, one above the writing desk, the other over the mantel, highlighting the purpose of pictures to capture a viewpoint, make it an object of contemplation, amid the flux. Mirrors, of course, capture anything placed before them; likewise, there is very little to suggest a hierarchy in a Berggruen painting. Everything is equal under the watchful eye of the artist and clock. Everything is equal, and anything is possible. Artist and clock conspire to persuade the viewer that pictures allow anyone to voyage across aeons simply by engaging, imaginatively, with a modest rectangle. For a moment, at least.

Looking at paintings such as *Song of the Water Rail* (2025) and *Appoggiatura* (2025), it's clear that Berggruen delights in taking the viewer for a playful ride through history. Both paintings depict anachronistic figures inhabiting a version of the present day, as if the artist placed them there to serve some kind of purpose. Despite its faintly Eastern-European backdrop and a typically van Gogh-esque canopy of clouds, Berggruen based the setting of *Song of the Water Rail* on Zurich, a lacustrine city replete with waterfowl. Relaxing among the birds is a figure lifted from a Tintoretto painting. The young man is all quiet focus and internality in the face of the eponymous bird squawking next to him. Two ducks to the left glance over, looking slightly perplexed or even annoyed. Note how the whole world appears unplaceable in time and location yet, from the sky to the water to the ducks, everything roils with a vigorous life force. The young man – holding a copy of *Marsh Lands*, presumably a reference to André Gide's metafictional novel *Marshlands*, which happens to feature a duck hunt – rests imperturbably, yet out of time, a spectre transplanted into the scene. A similar mood infuses *Appoggiatura*, with a young man, dressed as if from the eighteenth century, leaning into the landscape, with the effervescent swirl of colour in the sky an extension of his mind at work. Whether proxies for the artist or the viewer, these young men are both perceivers and creators: they read, make notes, think, concoct, enacting a flow of mutually transforming energies, from environment to inner life and vice versa.

A book-toting dandy also appears in the full-length portrait *Pocket Guide to British Birds* (2025). The book itself is the still point of an otherwise swirling picture, the protagonist's thumb firmly placed over the cover bird's wings as if preventing it from flying away. Berggruen was struck by the *contrapposto* energy of the figure in a portrait by the English painter Francis Cotes (1726–70), which she deployed here in a landscape that is so painterly it verges on the abstract. Although the landscape behind the figure is wildly connotative, full of deep blues and greens, and marked by ochre and crimson, the tones and colours are too subdued to merit the epithet expressionist. There is nevertheless an almost childlike delight in the power of brush and colour to enchant the eye, whatever the subject matter. Another take on an art-historical precedent, this time from a painting by Peter Paul Rubens, *Diana, Goddess of the Hunt and of the Forest* (2025) reinvents Diana as an Orphic figure, with birds circling her among the branches like singers in a choir. She is accompanied by a hound, that leaps on her thigh hoping she might toss the blue ball in her hand. Rather than hunting stags, they are out for an innocent walk among the flowers, as if playing a game of fetch in the Napa Valley. Just as Renaissance painters placed Biblical scenes in the familiar environs of Tuscan villages, Berggruen transposes art-historical figures into a landscape familiar to her, and her viewers. It's worth pointing out how the composition and palette of *Diana, Goddess of the Hunt and of the Forest* echoes another work, *Path Work, Luxembourg Gardens* (2013–25), a painting of a red digger in Paris's famously exquisite, and neo-classical, jardin. In Berggruen's imagination, workers are also gods.

The setting of *Suspension of the Future Tense* (2025) is a room laced with vibrant ghosts. The wallpaper bursts forth as a lush, Rousseau-like jungle, a window opens wide to reveal what looks to be a Mediterranean landscape, while a mirror to its left introduces a different perspective, a fragment of another window. A dog, resting contentedly, lies beside a chair that looks as if it's just been pushed away from the table upon which rests a book that shares the title of the painting, apparently written by the great art historian TJ Clark. The cover of the book features a key figure from Poussin's *Landscape with a Man Killed by a Snake* (1648), the man fleeing in terror from the grisly scene described by the title. Clark's book focusing on *Landscape with a Man Killed by a Snake* is in fact called *Sight of Death: An Experiment in Art Writing*, a long, diaristic essay about looking slowly and repeatedly at two Poussin landscapes. Berggruen lets her imagination rewrite the book, thus introducing her own philosophy to the room: 'suspension of the future tense' might be a good epithet for the artist's overall vision. A survey of Berggruen's recent body of work indicates how deeply and heavily her perception and depiction of the world are inflected by both the history of image-making and the power of paint to suspend, or even reinvent, time, at least as we apprehend a picture. And yet the paintings are loaded with reminders of WH Auden's phrase, 'O let not Time deceive you, / You cannot conquer Time', two memorable lines from his magisterial song

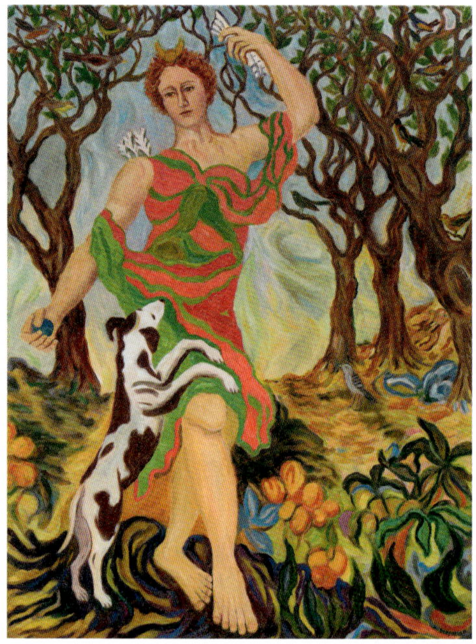

Diana, Goddess of the Hunt and of the Forest, 2025
Oil on linen
101.6 × 76.2 cm
40 × 30 in

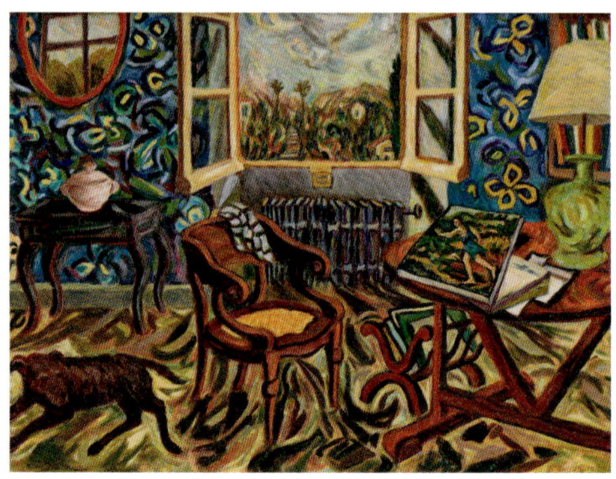

Suspension of the Future Tense, 2025
Oil on linen
76.2 × 101.6 cm
30 × 40 in

'As I Walked Out One Evening'. Poems and paintings admonish us to keep both a respectful eye on the clock and a loving eye on our past and our future. Everywhere Berggruen's canvases are alive with reminders that 'life remains a blessing', as Auden declares later in the poem.

A relatively small picture, *Verlaine's Verses* (2025) is vast and generous in spirit. A multifarious swoon of orange flowers dominates the painting, topped by a window that frames a chimney-tickled sky of creamy marble. On the lower left, a book cracked open to a fisherman framed by the limpid blue brushstrokes of a body of water, probably a reproduction of a French Impressionist or post-Impressionist painting; to the bottom right, two lines from Paul Verlaine's poem (or song) 'Mandoline', seemingly written in fresh ink – the bottle a nod to Berggruen's affection for outmoded forms of communication. The sky of the painting-within-the-painting is continuous in tone and hue with the sky in the window, while the greenish-yellow wall is as vividly alive as anything in this work. The two lines from Verlaine – descriptions of clothes – are arguably the most mundane in the whole poem, a choice that somehow divulges something about Berggruen's worldview. Art isn't always or only about grand things and transcendence. The page sings, the wall sings, the chimneys dance across the canvas like notes on a score. I titled this essay 'Everyday Enchantments' intuitively as I started to write. It was only when I had almost finished that I remembered that 'to enchant' means to fill with song. I'd inadvertently tapped into Berggruen's own title, *The Song Inside of Things*, which she adapted from Joseph Freiherr von Eichendorff's famous poem 'Wünschelrute', or 'dowsing rod', with its proverbial line, 'A song sleeps in all things'.

A beautiful idea, everywhere manifested in Berggruen's work. The line from the poem reminded me of one from a letter that van Gogh wrote to his brother: 'the best way to know God is to love many things'. Whatever van Gogh meant by 'God', his thought implies a radically non-hierarchical view of life, something I believe he shares with Berggruen. When we look at a painting by Berggruen, and van Gogh for that matter, we recognise the world, but we also see the artist's sensibility at work, layering her perception with art-historical allusions, memories and desires, while revelling in all the tactile delights of pigment and form. And with equal force we sense the artist articulating her view that every surface on the earth is alive, blessed with song, and therefore deserves our care and attention. In an era that so often swings from devout materialism, with tech bros hoping to freeze their flesh for some bleak eternity, to religious fundamentalism or even theocratic dogma, Berggruen's work is a reminder that as long as we're alive we can draw a song from a cloud, a stone or a goddess before they disappear forever. We can leave the world enchanted.

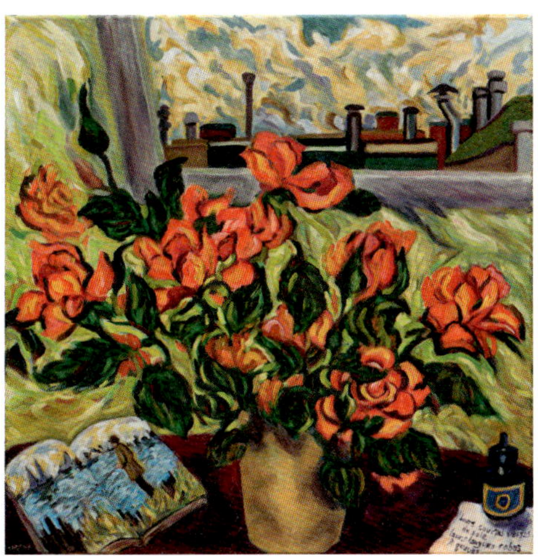

Verlaine's Verses, 2025
Oil on linen
61 × 61 cm
24 × 24 in

If, 2025
Oil on linen
61 × 61 cm
24 × 24 in

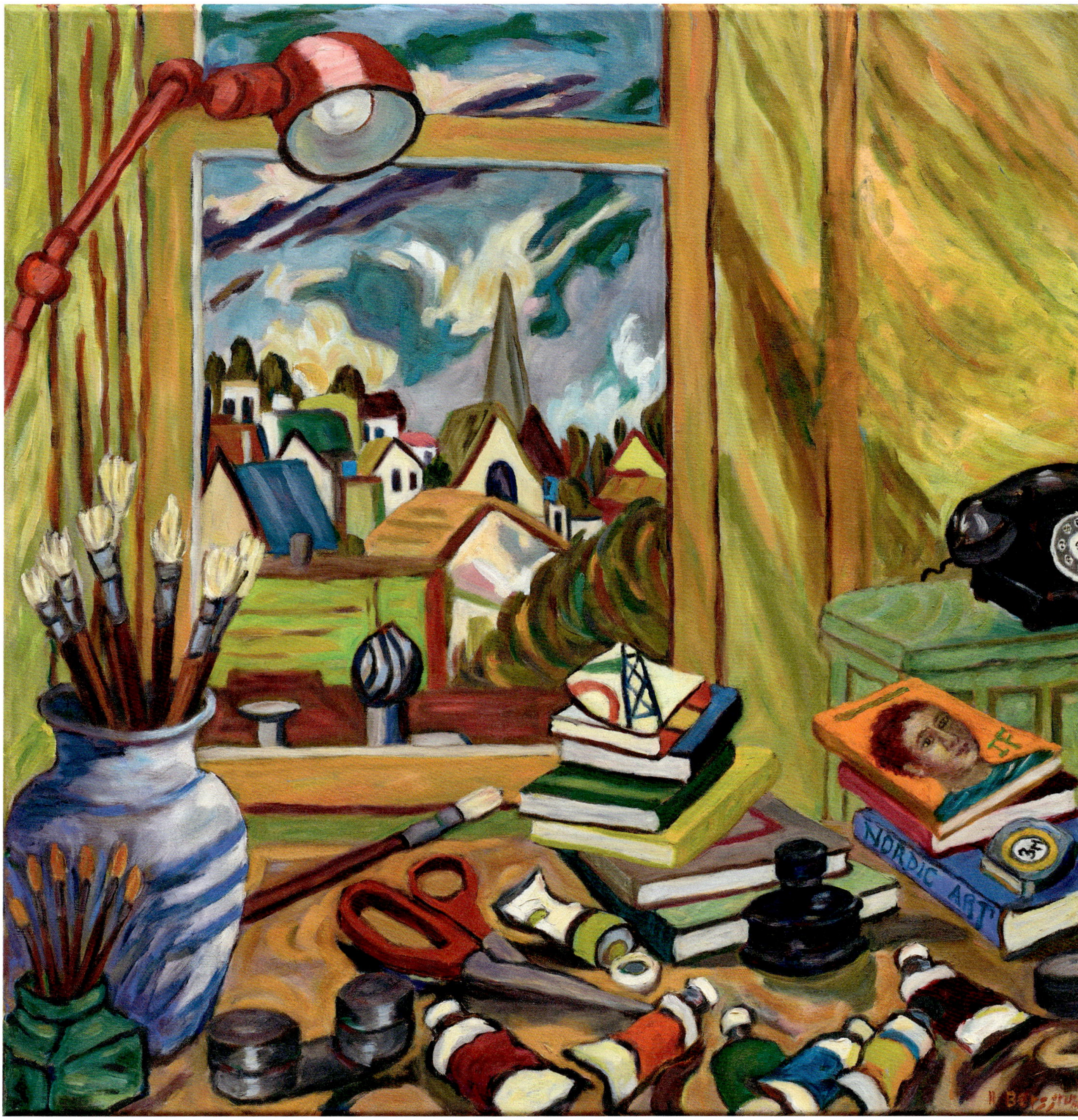
NORDIC ART

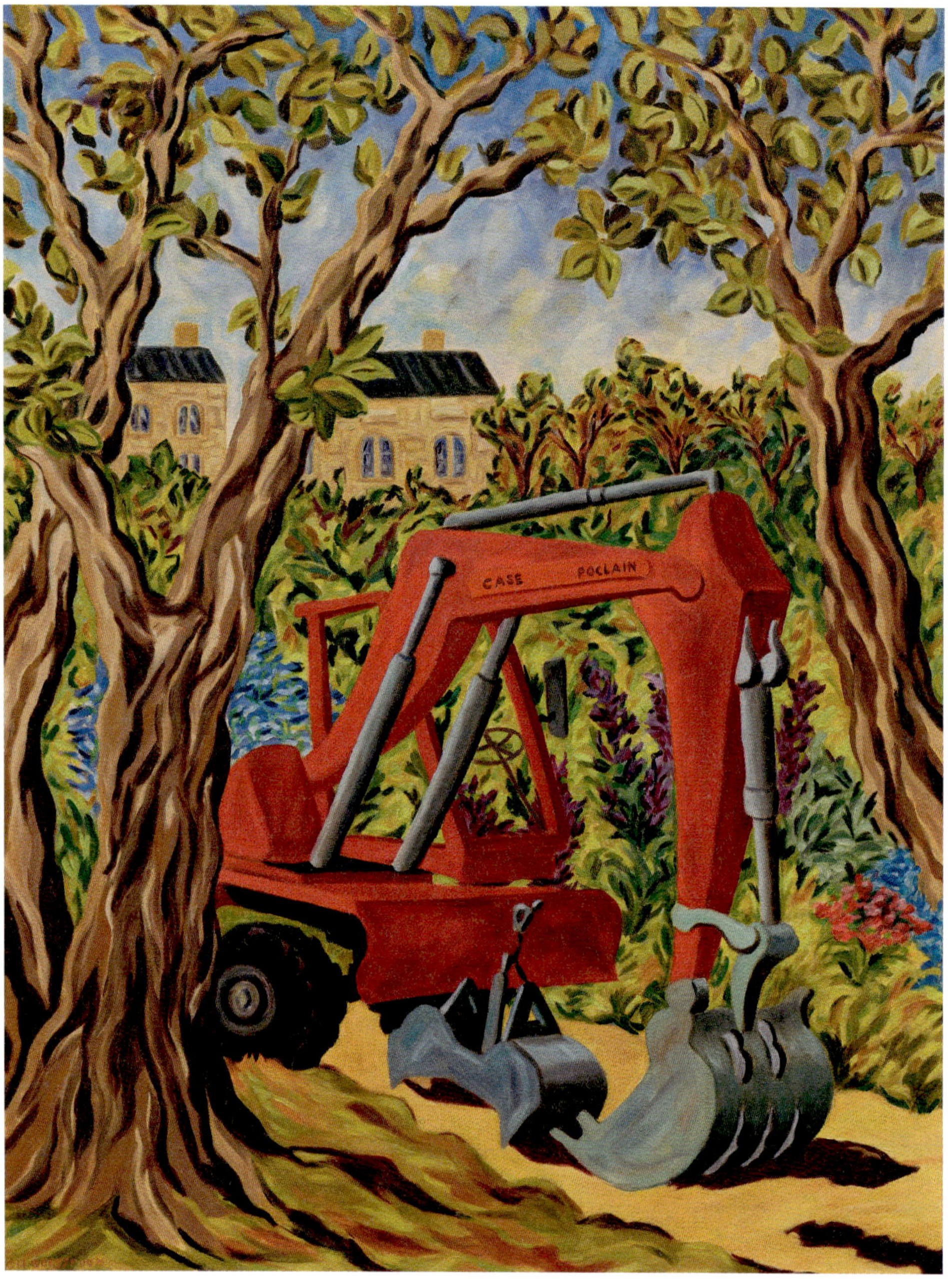

Path Work, Luxembourg Gardens, 2013–25
Oil on canvas
116.9 × 86.4 cm
46 × 34 in

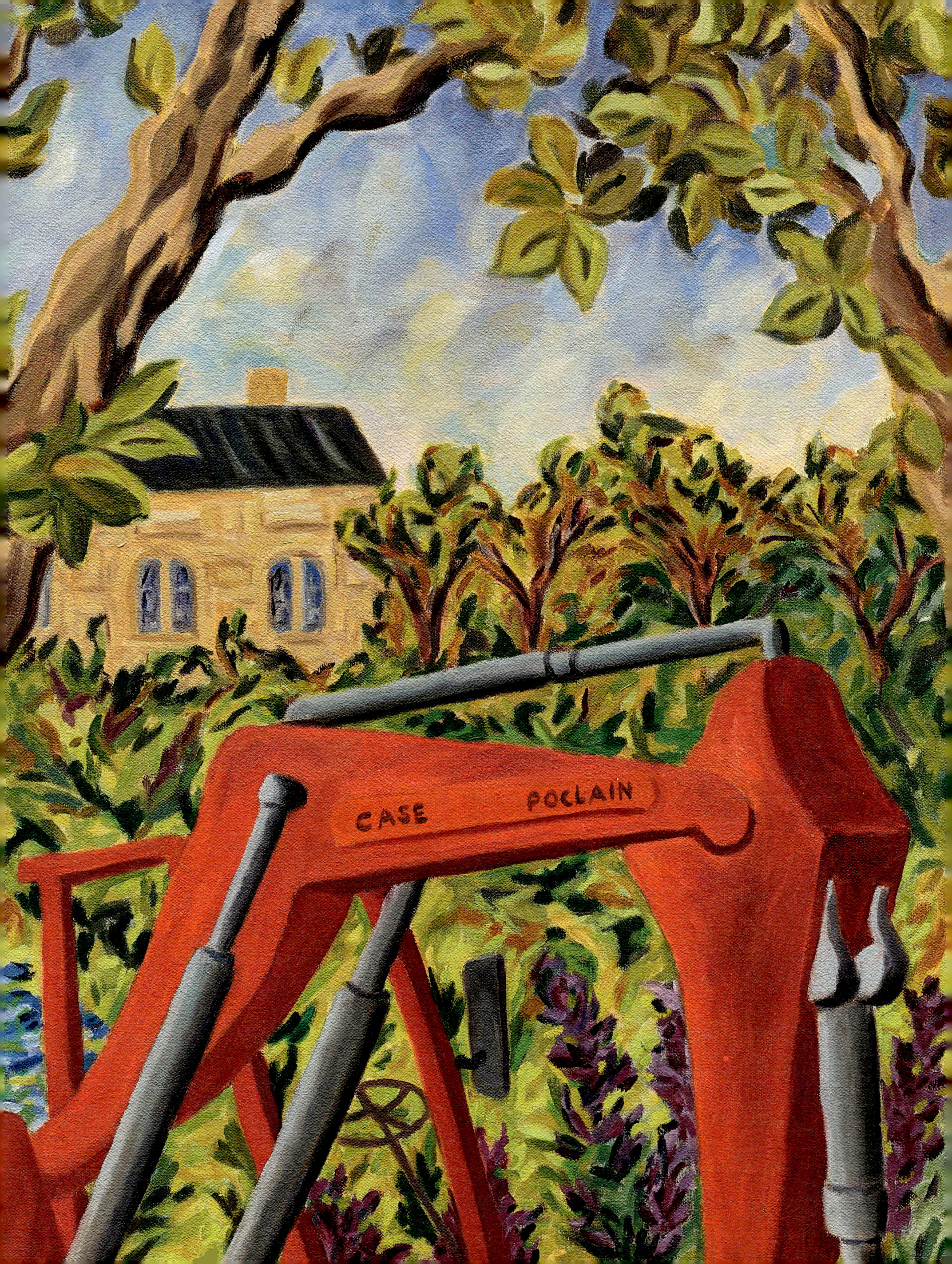
CASE
POCLAIN

Silos in Oxford, Iowa, 2005–25
Oil on linen
45.7 cm × 61 cm
18 × 24 in

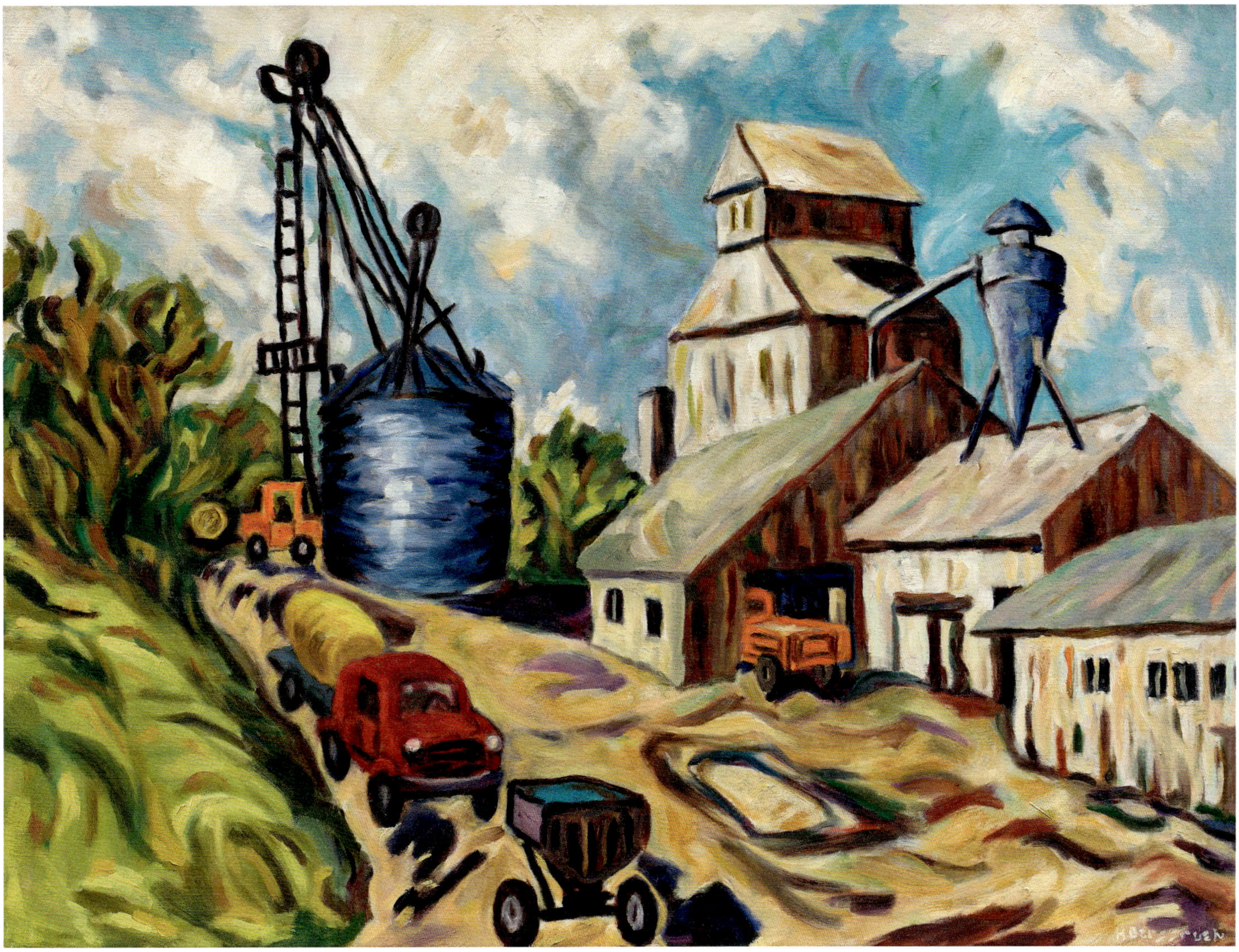

Elkader Co-op, 2005–25
Oil on linen
61 cm × 45.7 cm
24 × 18 in

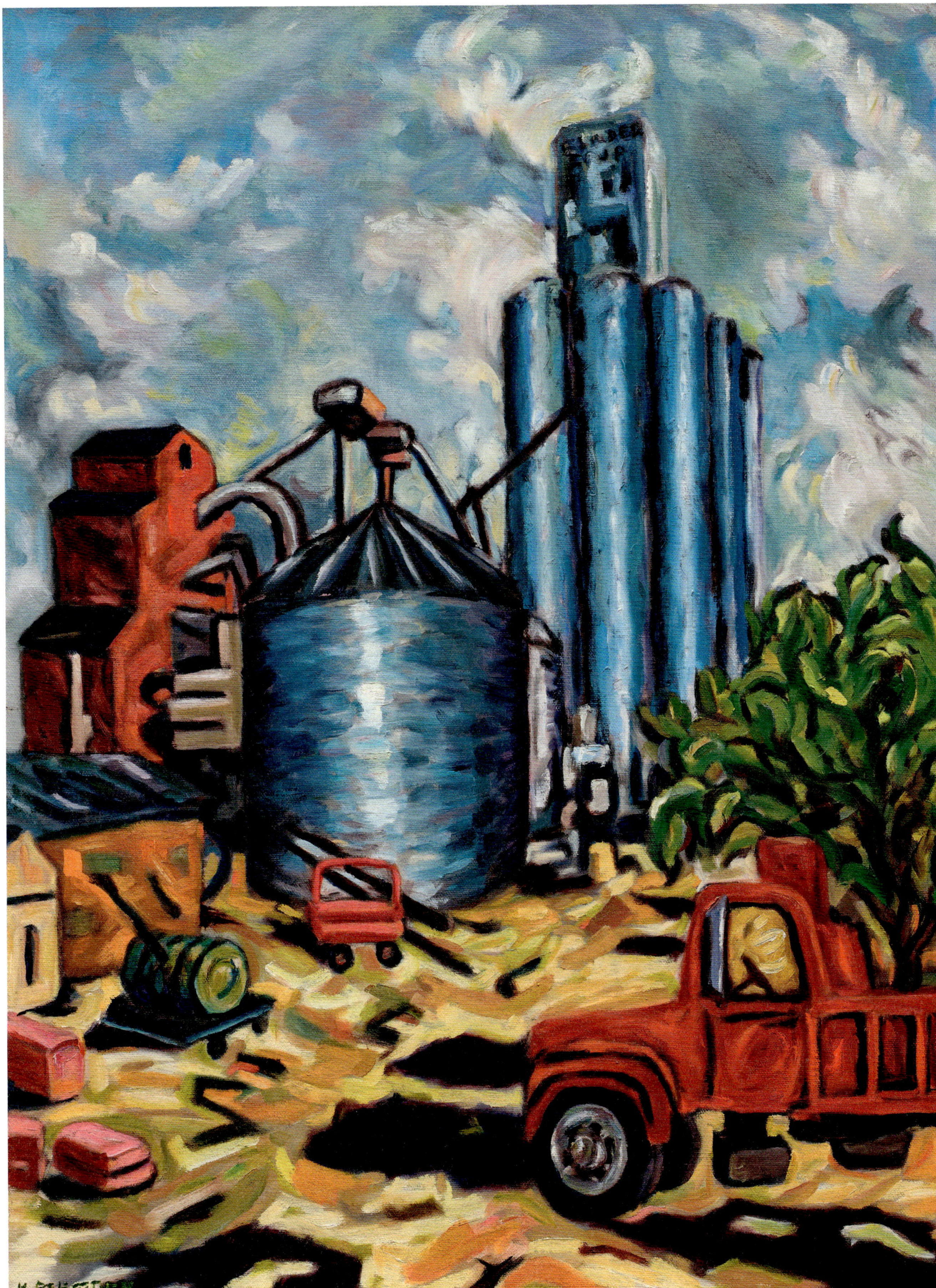

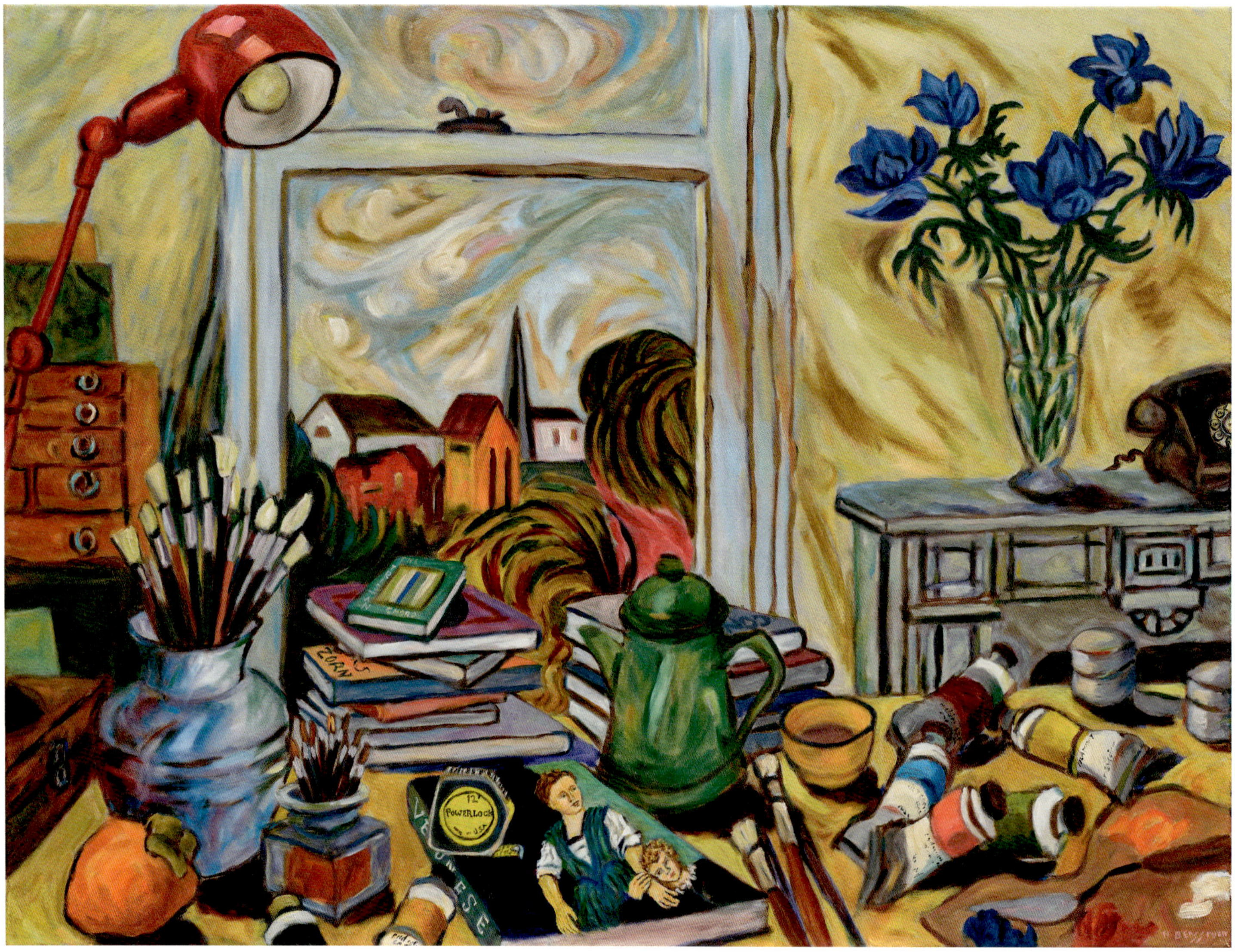

Powerlock, 2025
Oil on linen
76.2 × 101.6 cm
30 × 40 in

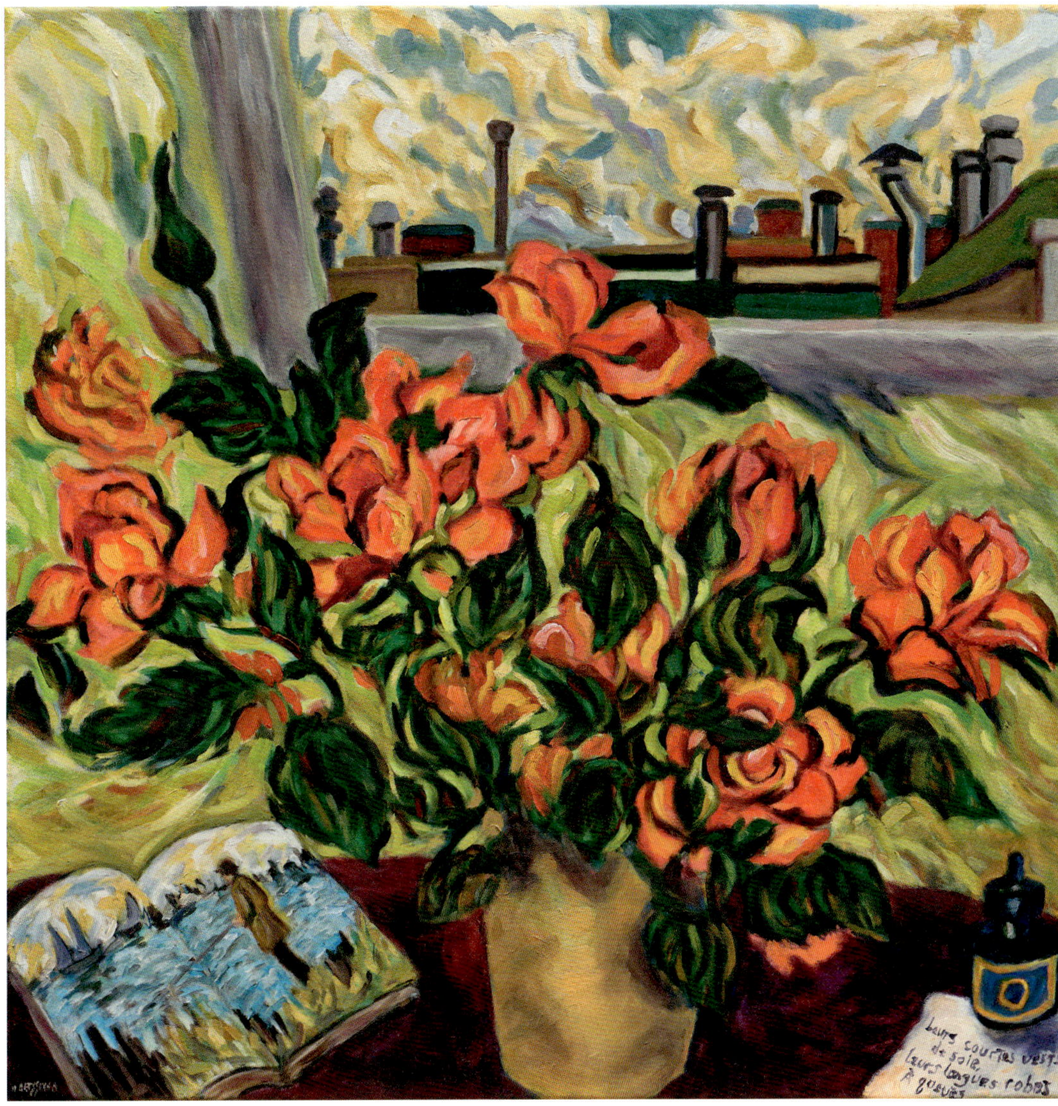

Verlaine's Verses, 2025
Oil on linen
61 × 61 cm
24 × 24 in

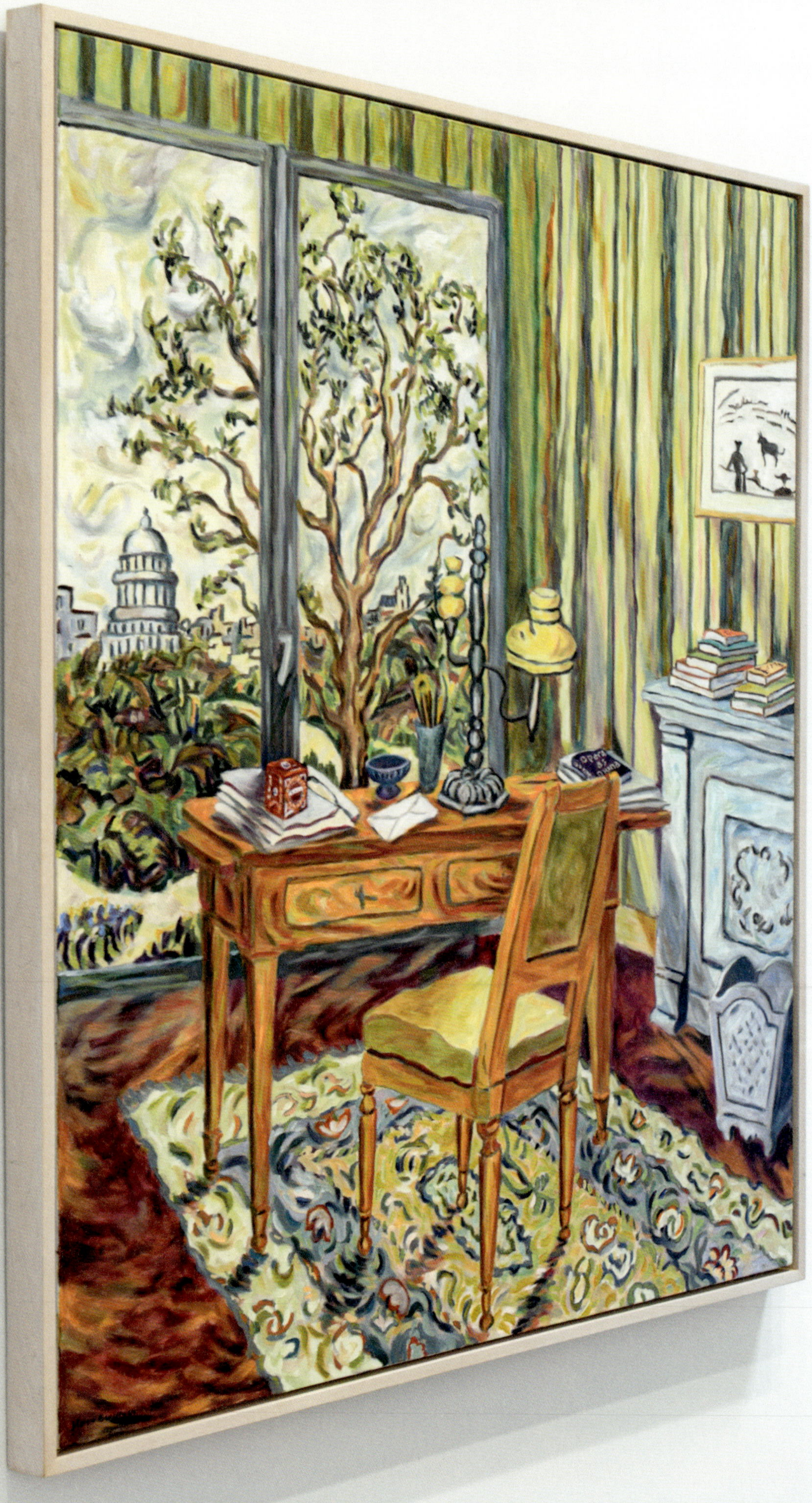

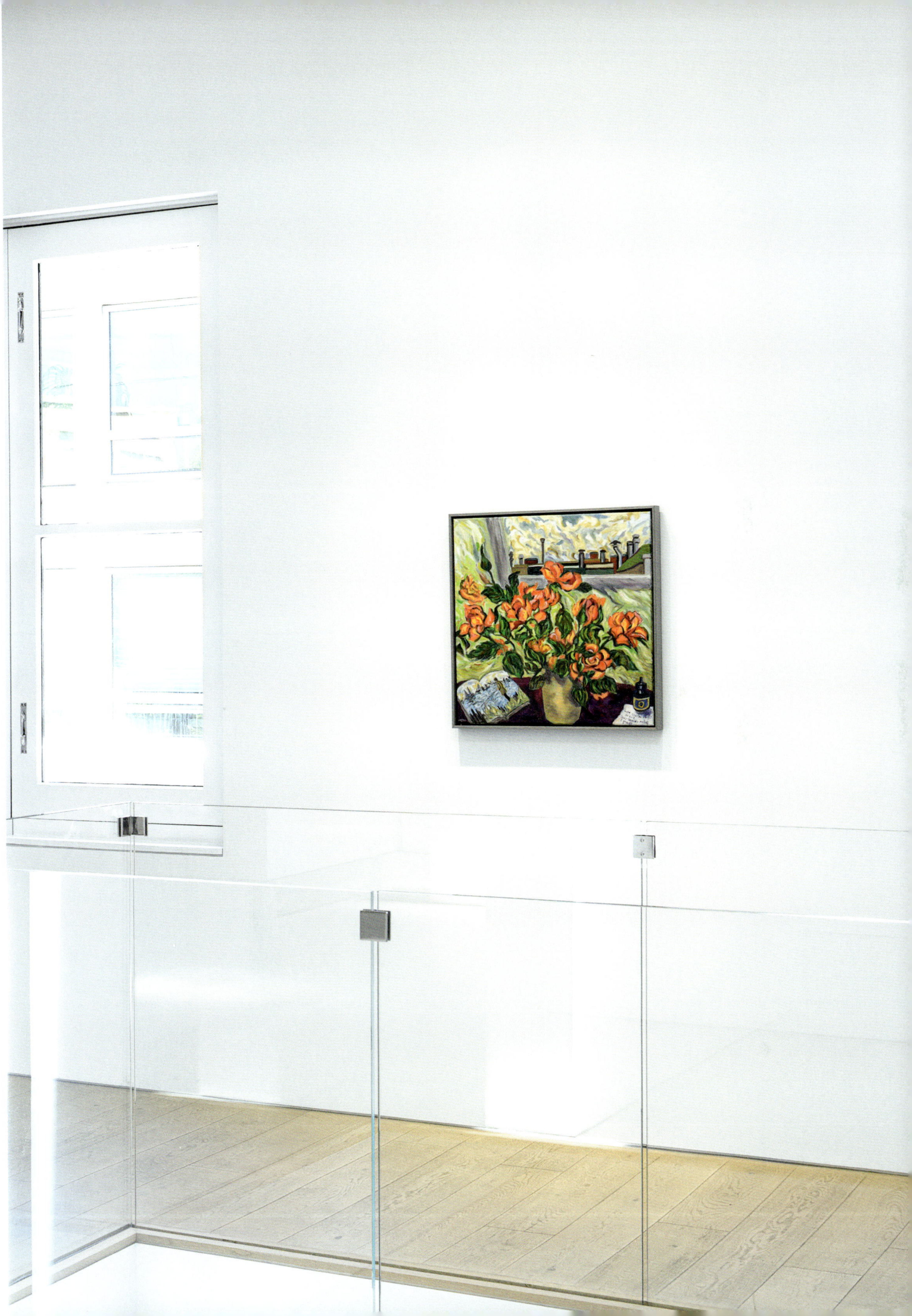

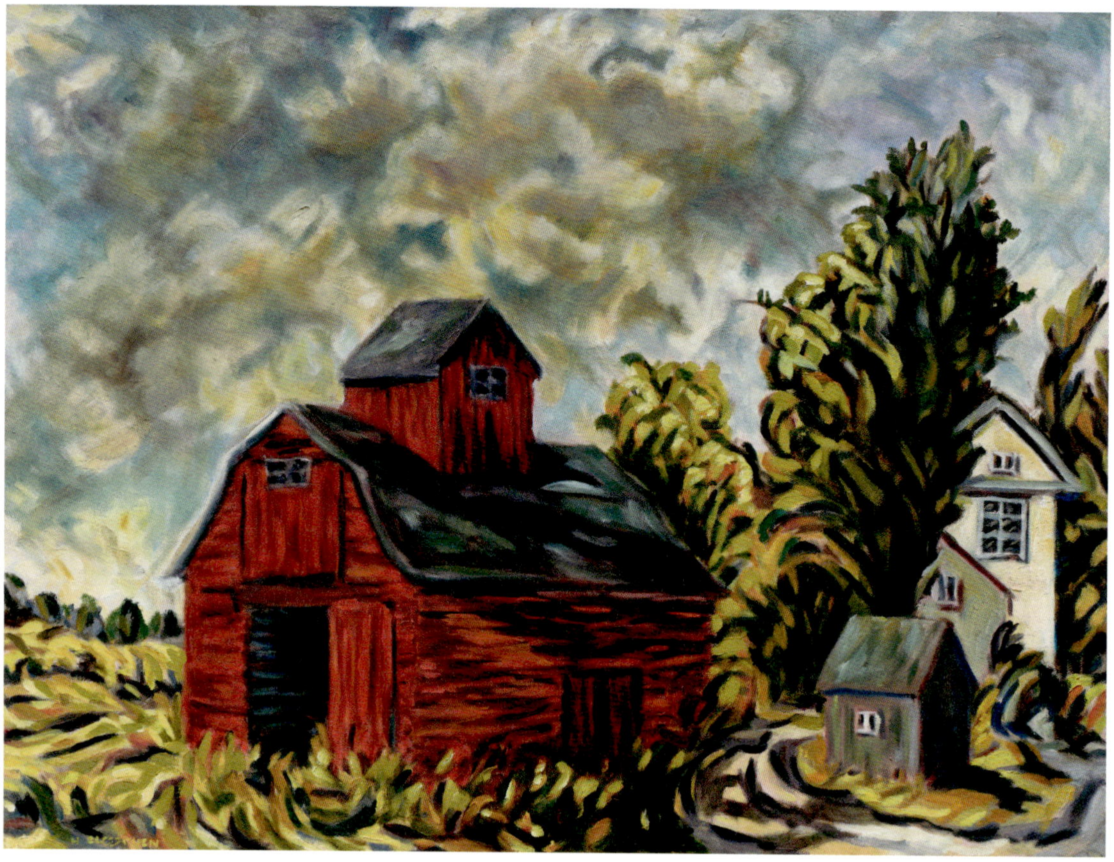

Red Barn, 2011
Oil on canvas
45.7 × 61cm
18 × 24 in

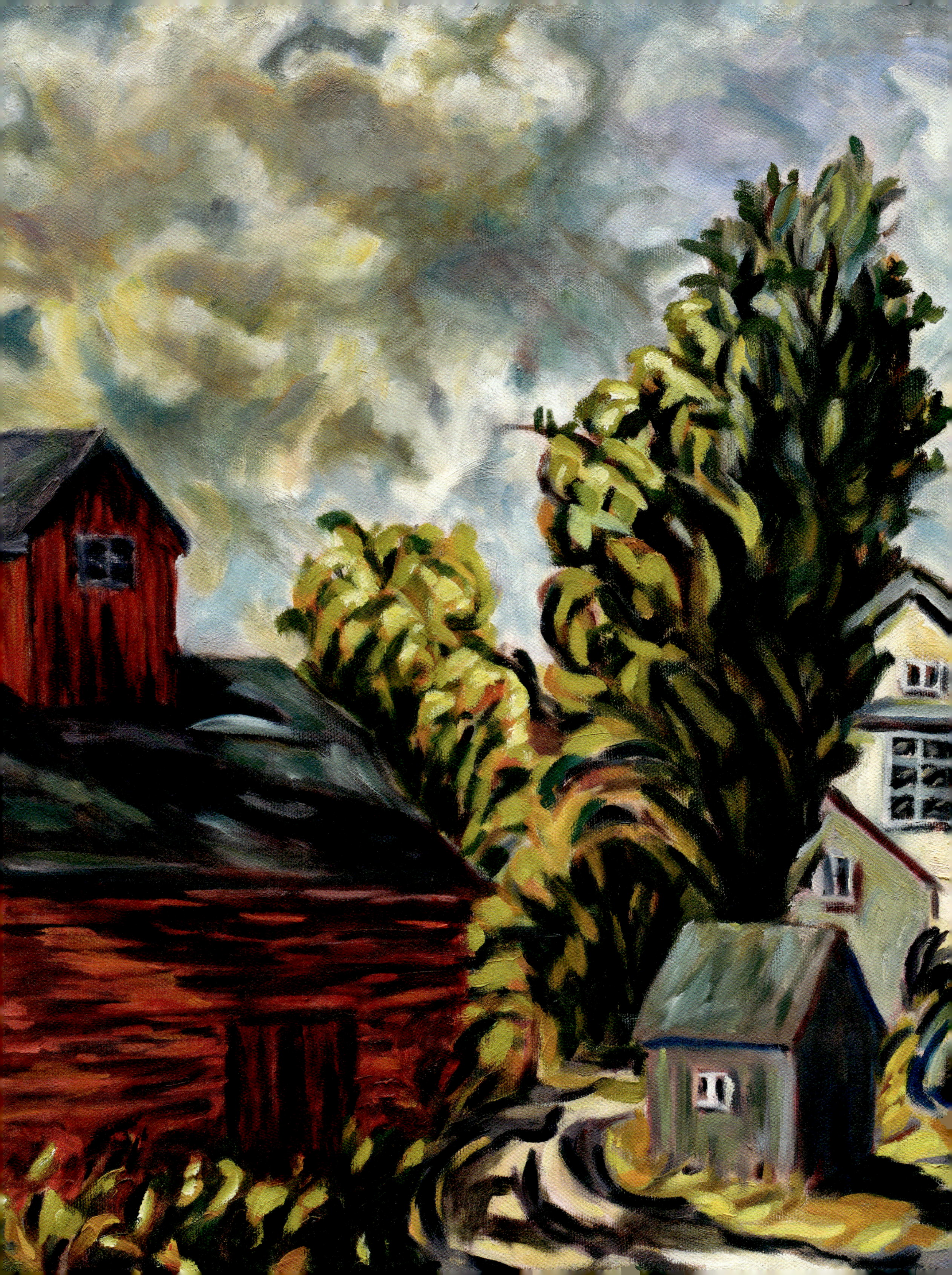

Schoolboy with Satchel, 2025
Oil on linen
71.1 × 55.9 cm
28 × 22 in

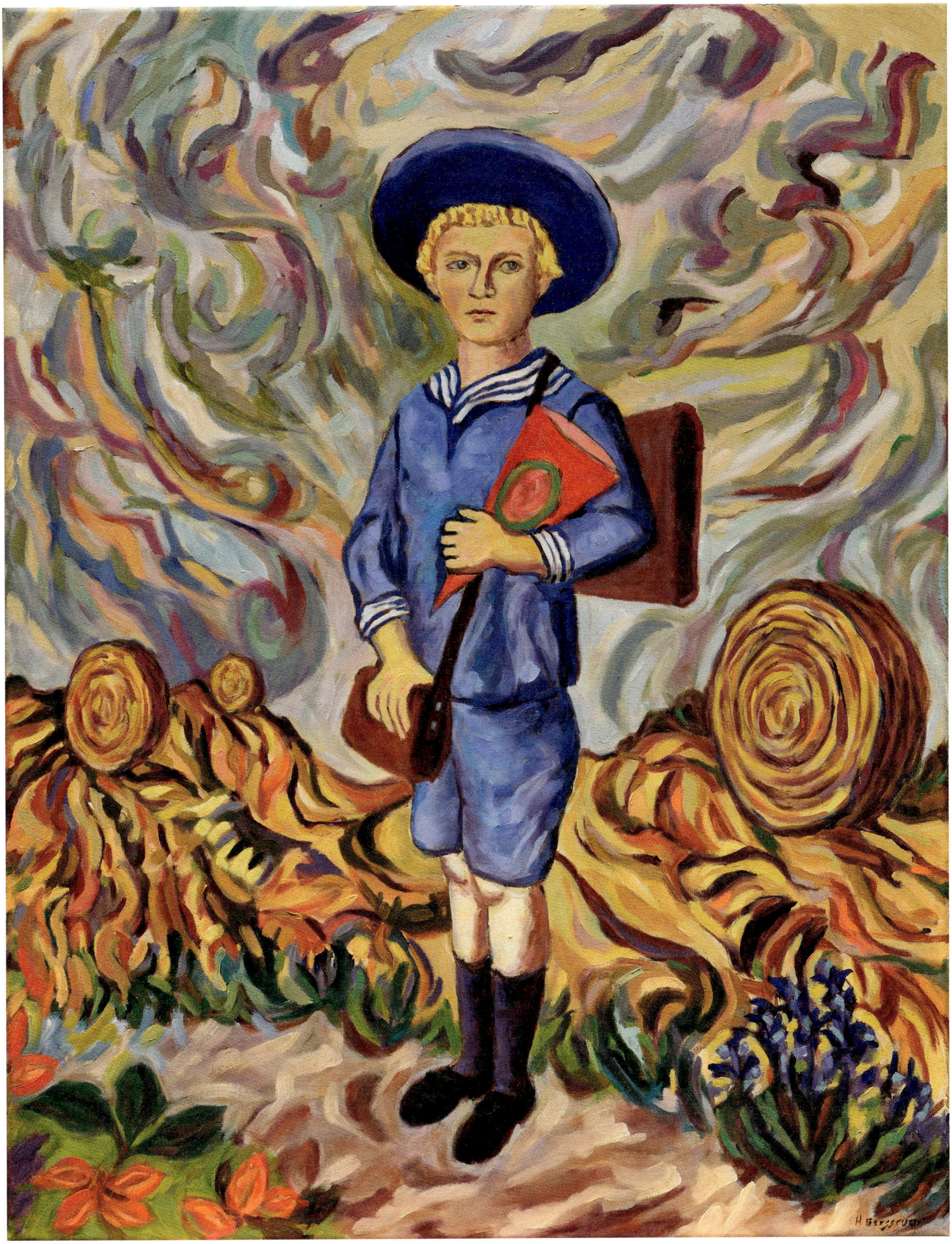

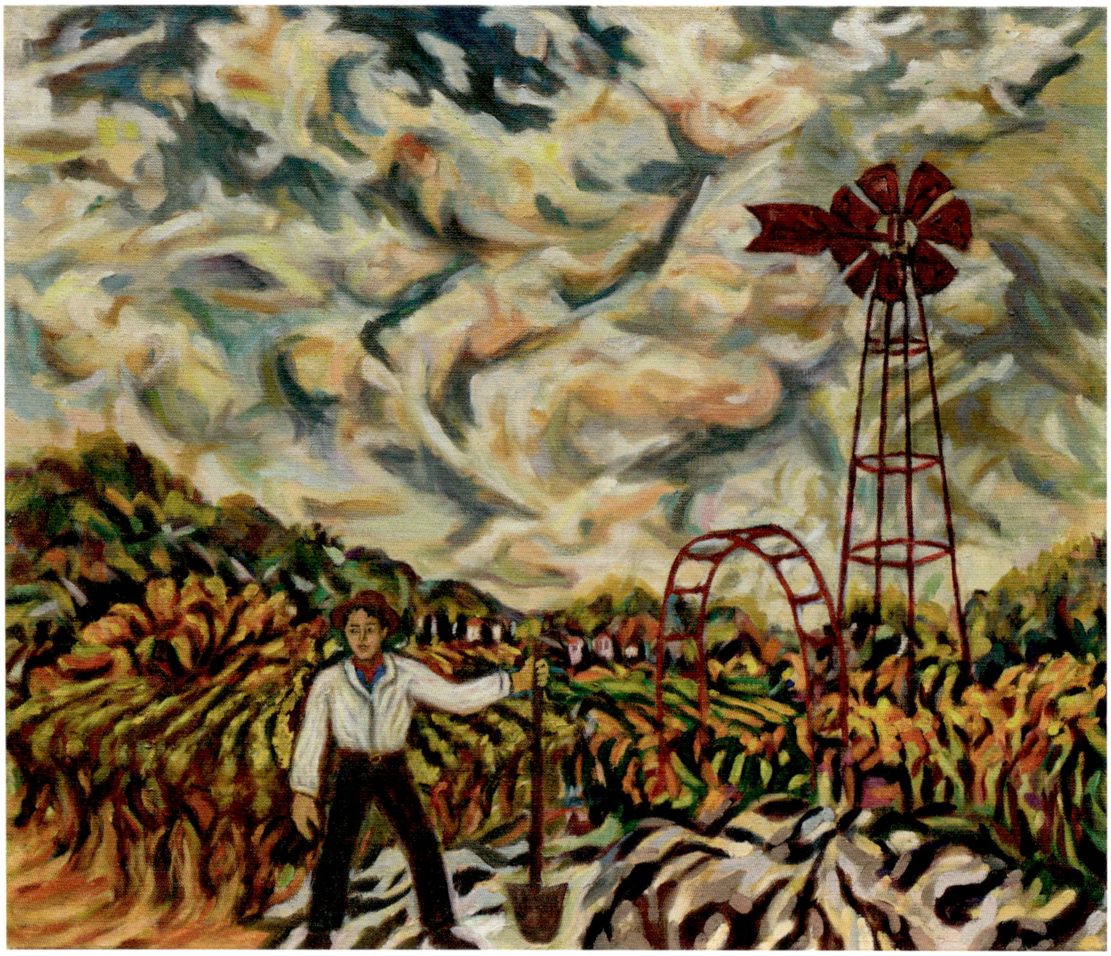

Vineyard Farm Hand, 2025
Oil on linen
50.8 × 60.7 cm
20 × 24 in

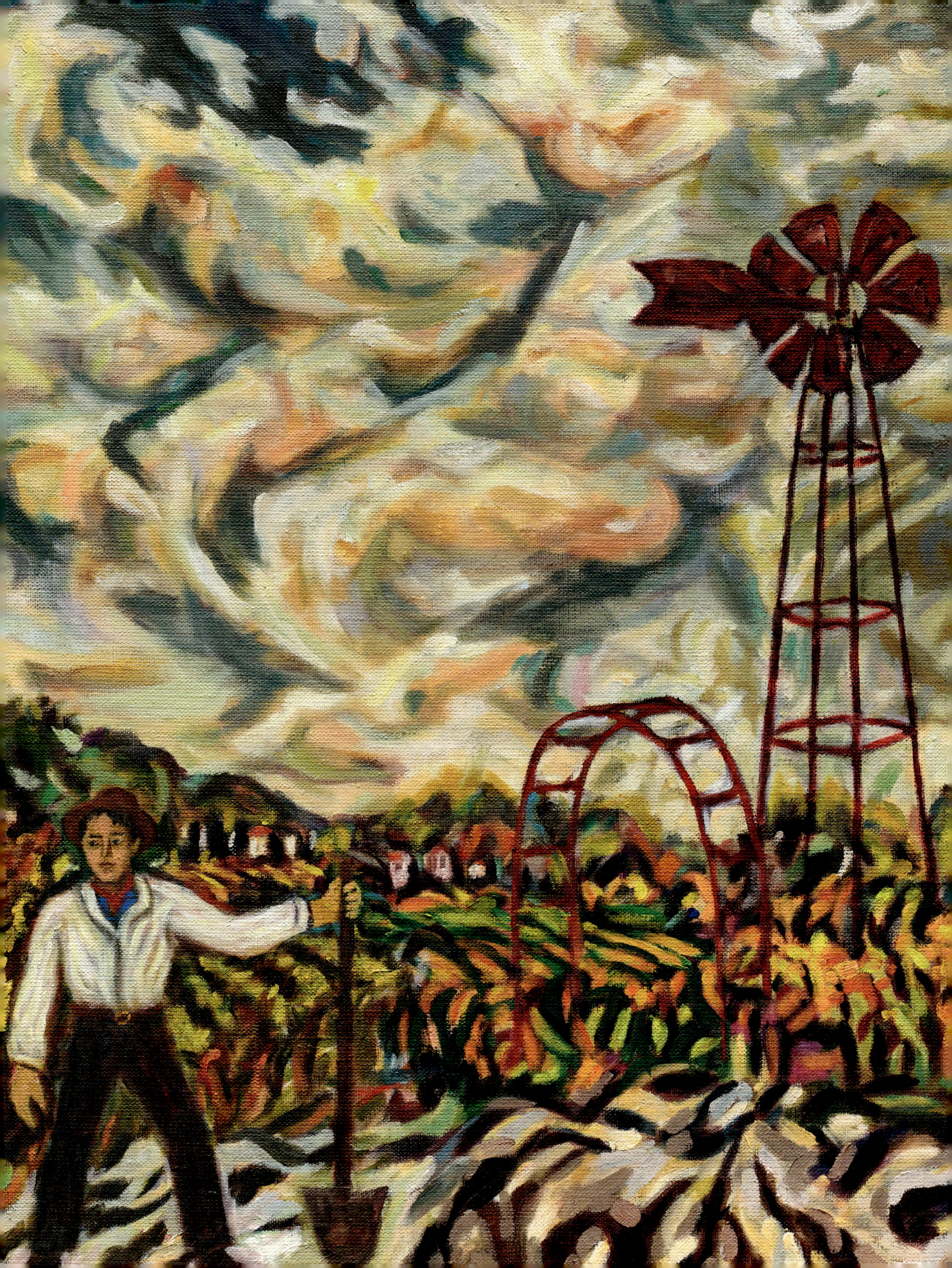

Interior with Matadors, 2018
Oil on linen
121.9 × 101.6 cm
48 × 40 in

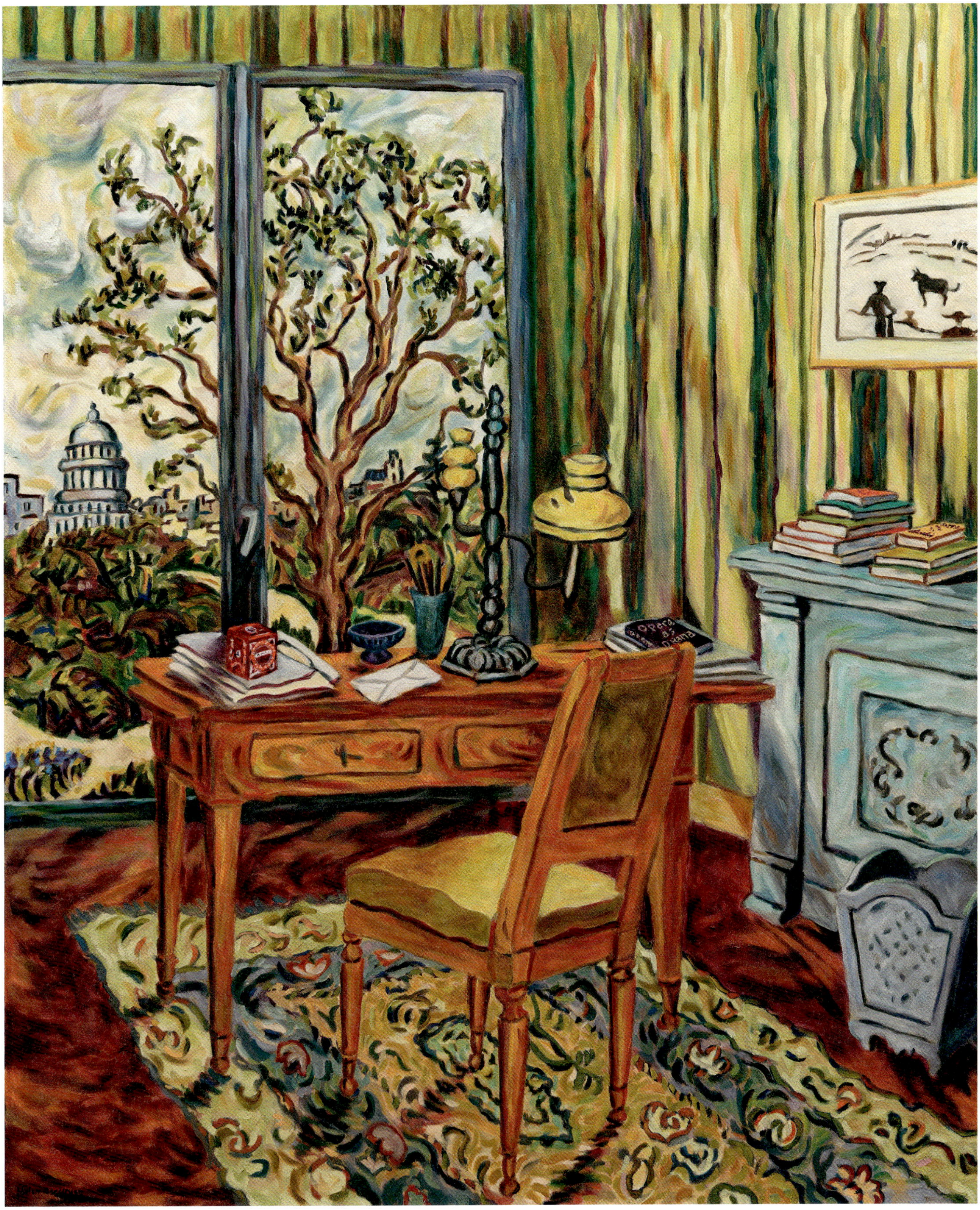

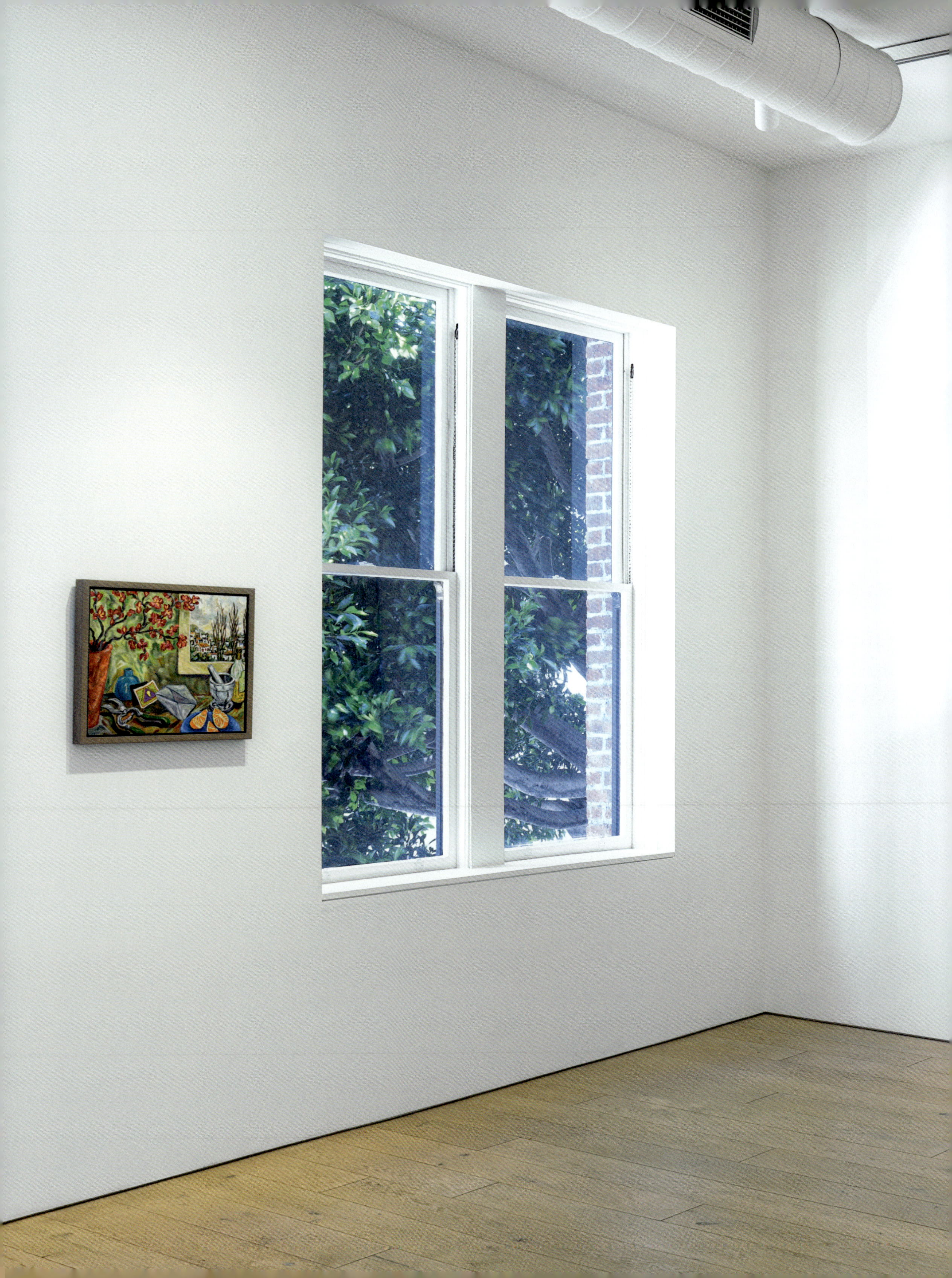

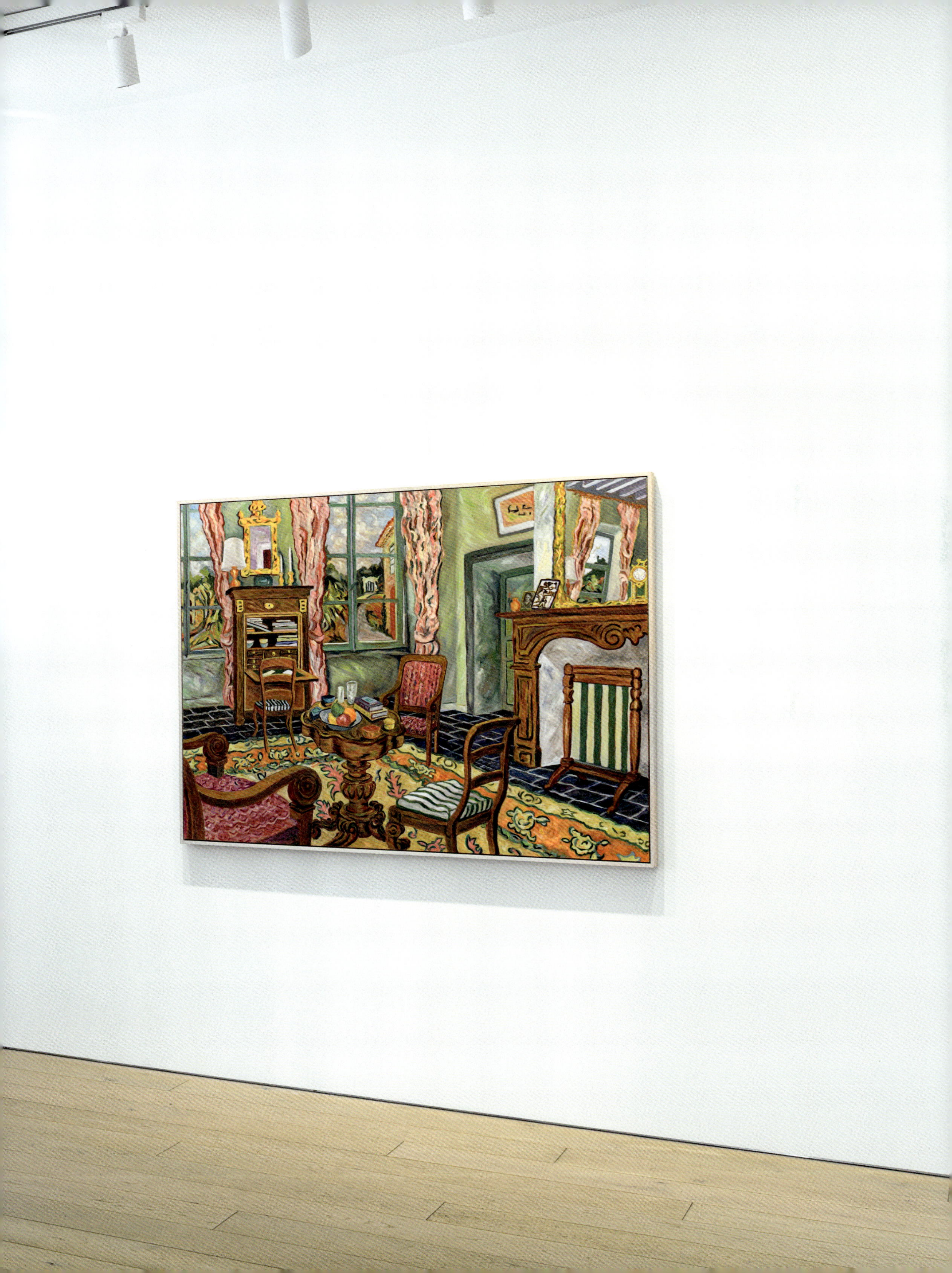

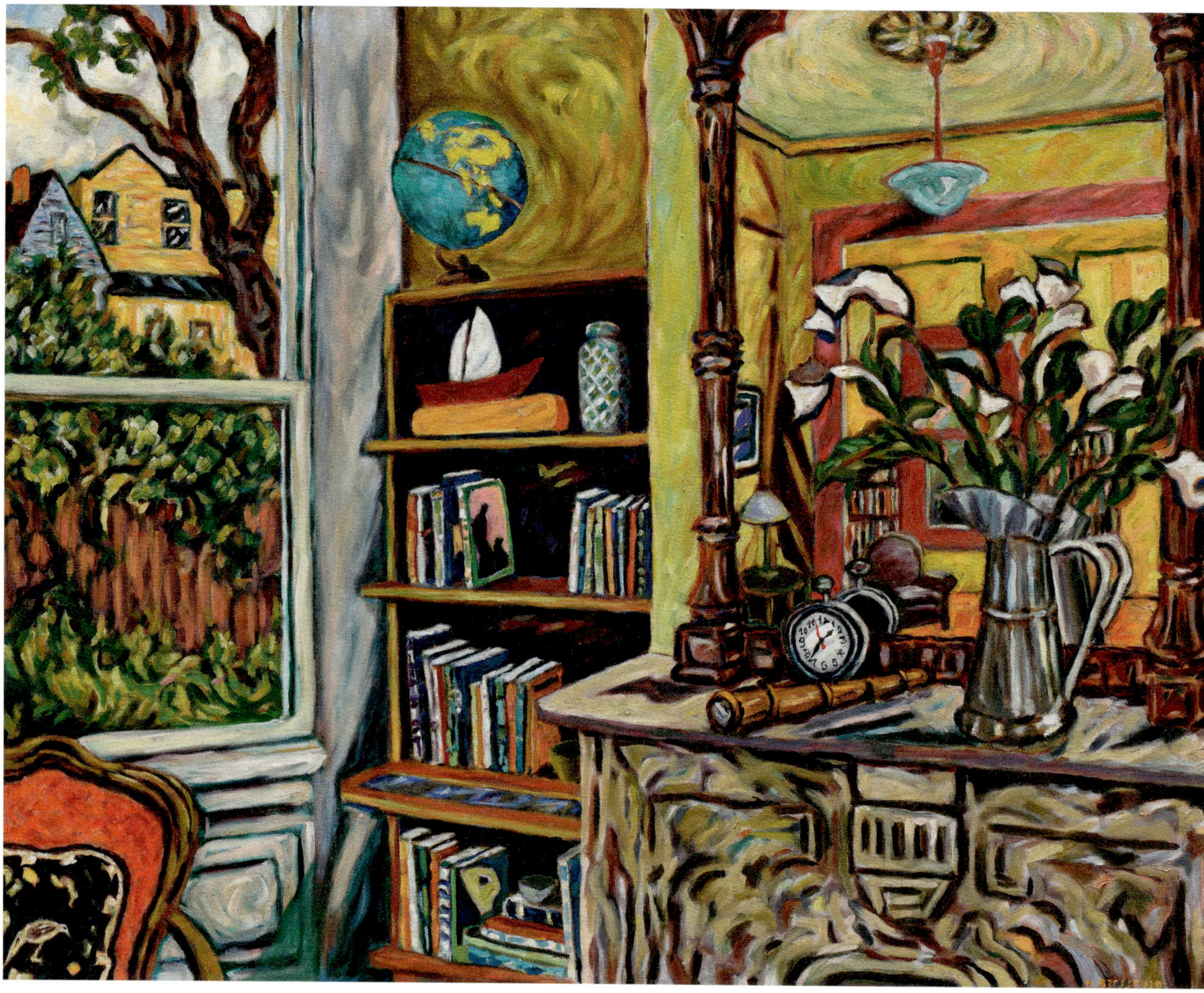

Mantel with Globe & Telescope, 2013–25
Oil on linen
55.9 × 71.1 cm
22 × 28 in

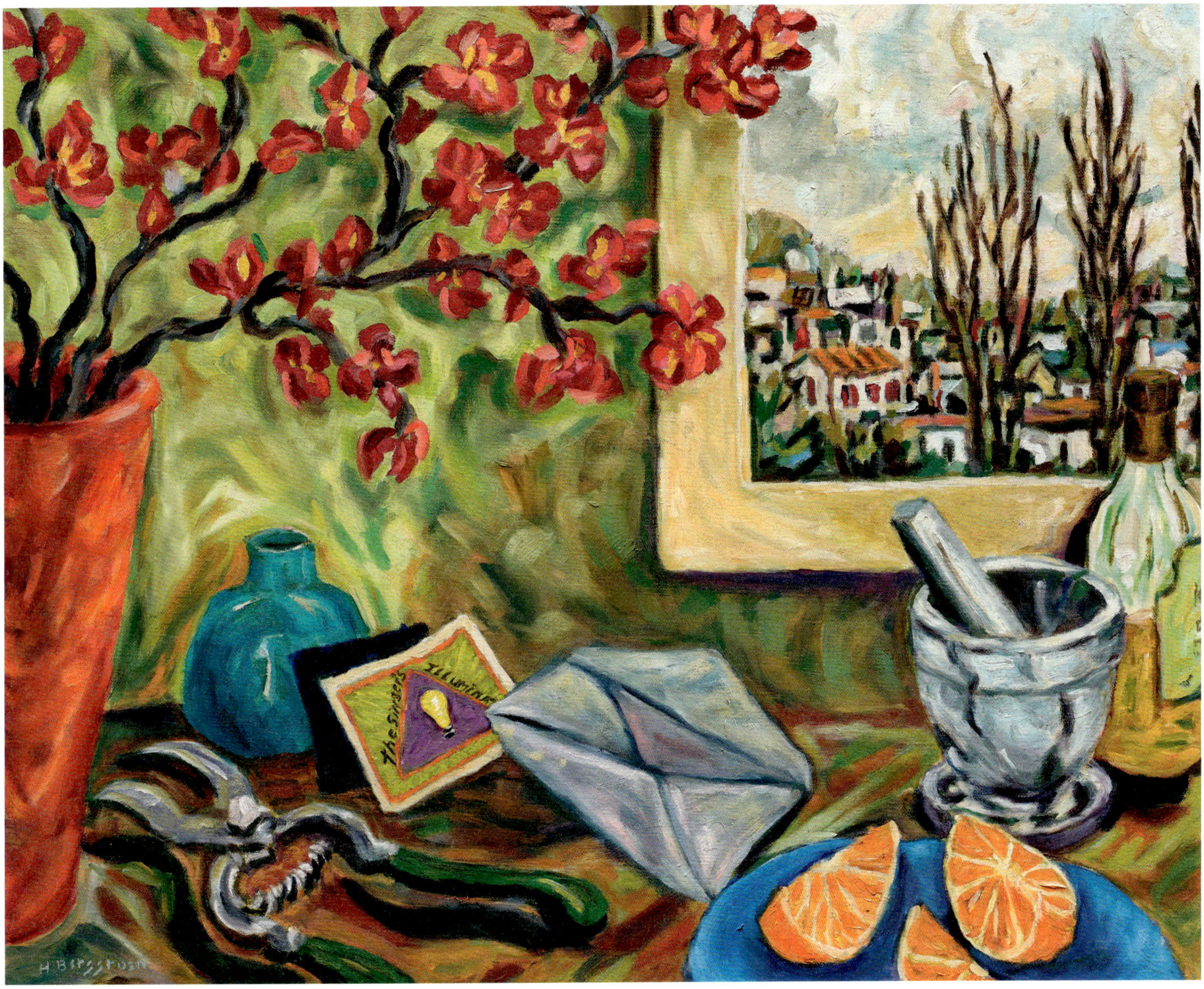

The Singer's Illuminations, 2012–15
Oil on linen
40.6 × 50.8 cm
16 × 20 in

Pocket Guide to British Birds, 2025
Oil on linen
101.6 × 76.2 cm
40 × 30 in

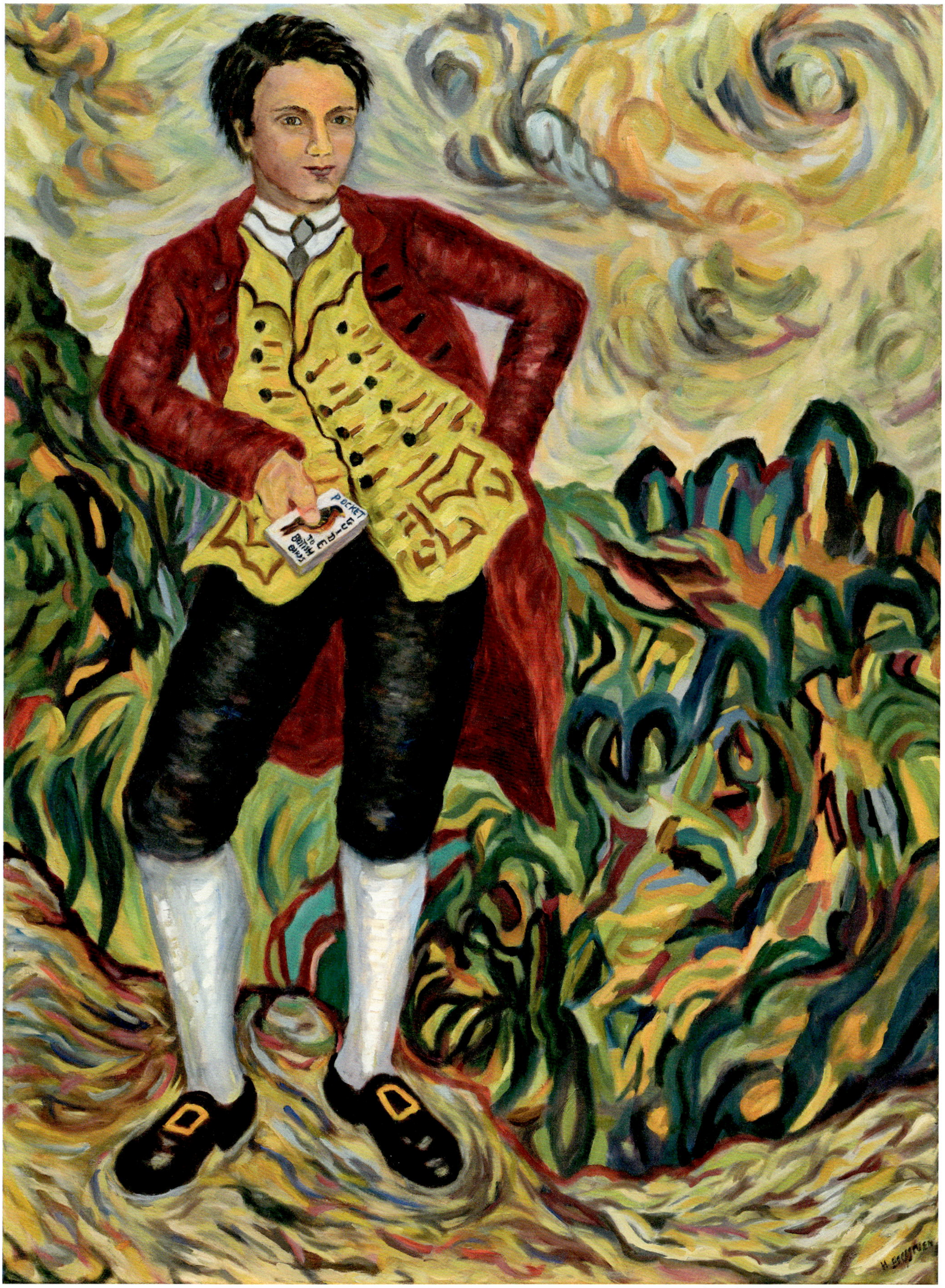
POCKET
GUIDE
TO
BRITISH
BIRDS

Three Cows, 2010–25
Oil on linen
45.7 cm × 61 cm
18 × 24 in

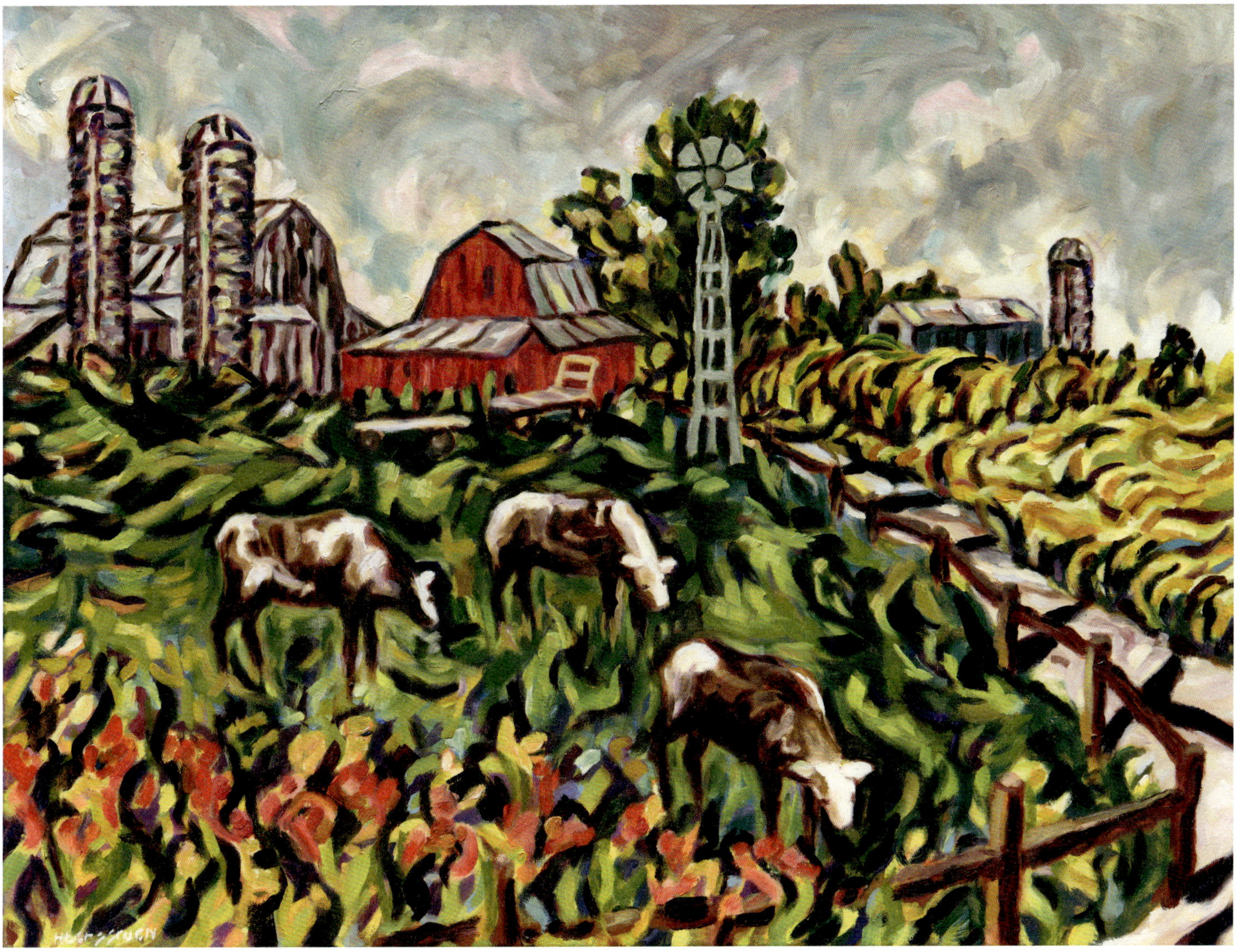

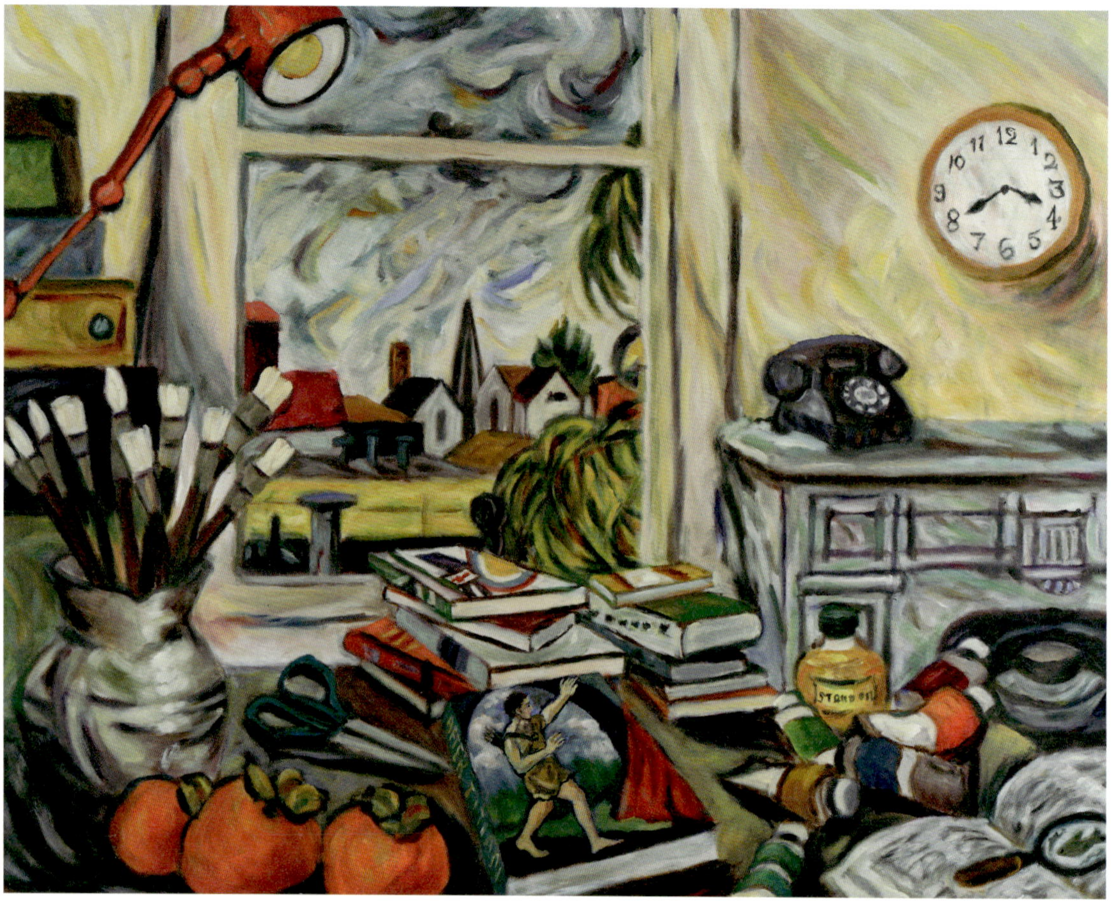

Actaeon, 2017
Oil on linen
55.9 × 71.1 cm
22 × 28 in

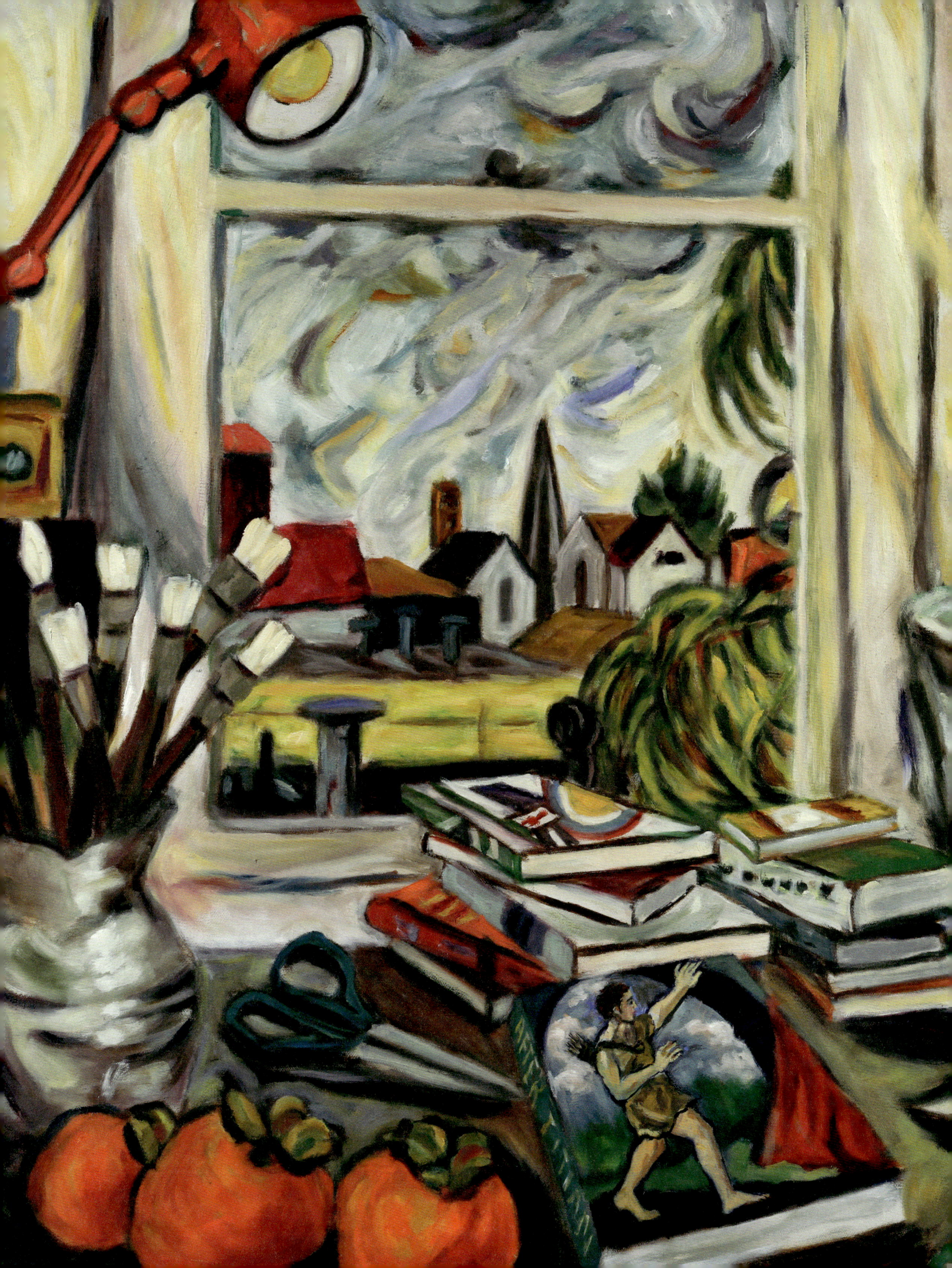

Fall Harvest with Open Book, 2018
Oil on canvas
71.1 cm × 91.4 cm
28 × 36 in

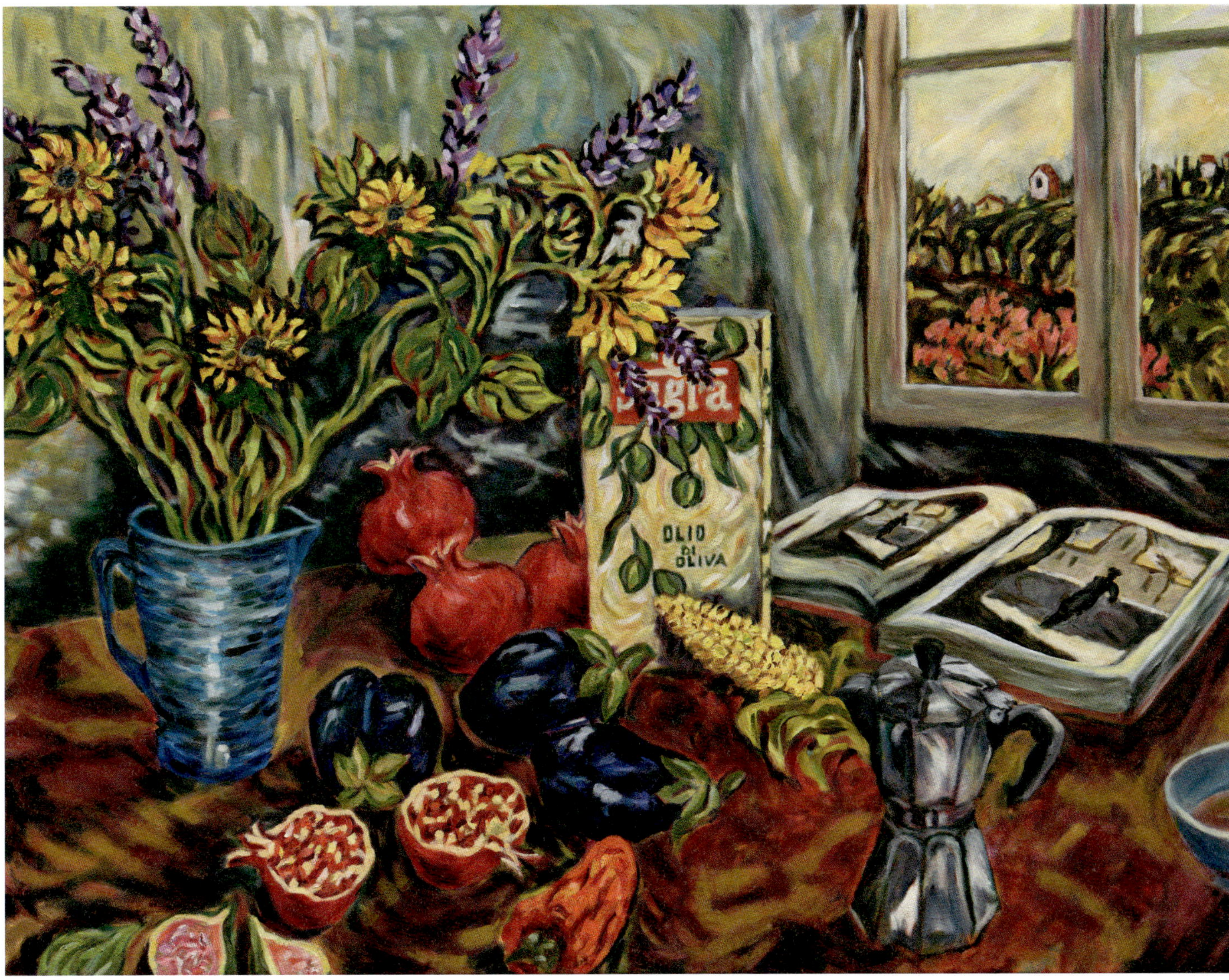
OLIO
DI
OLIVA

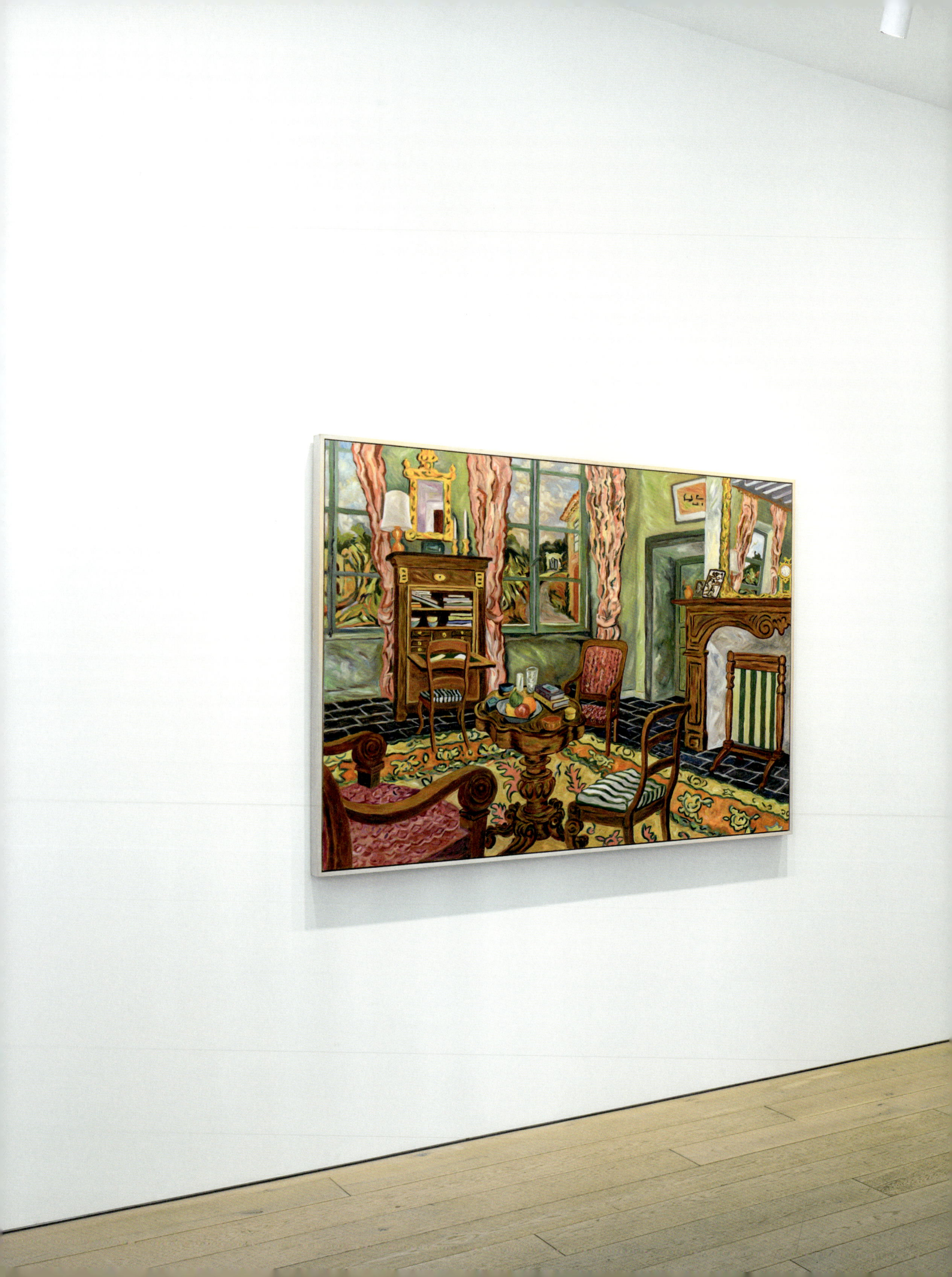

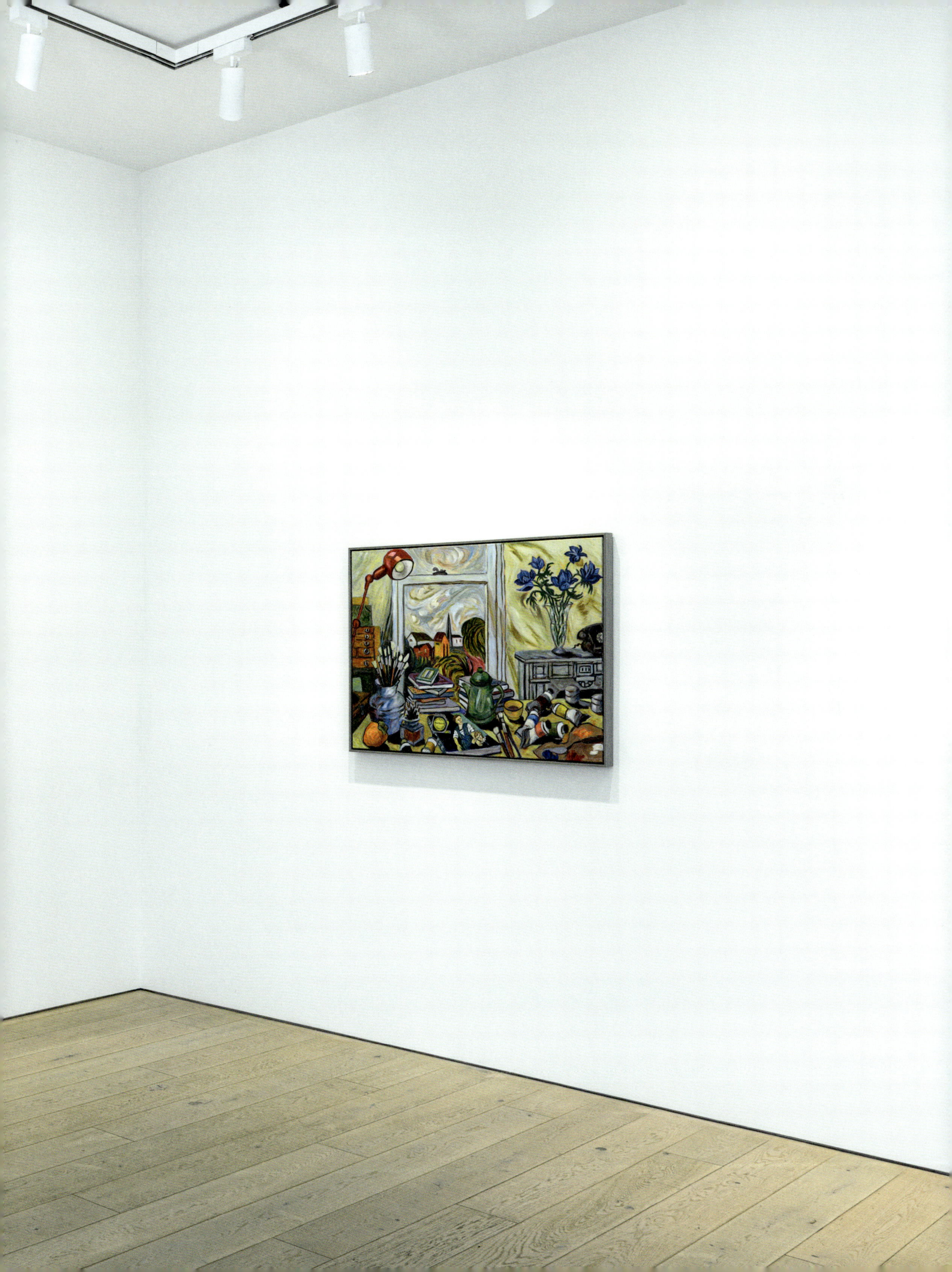

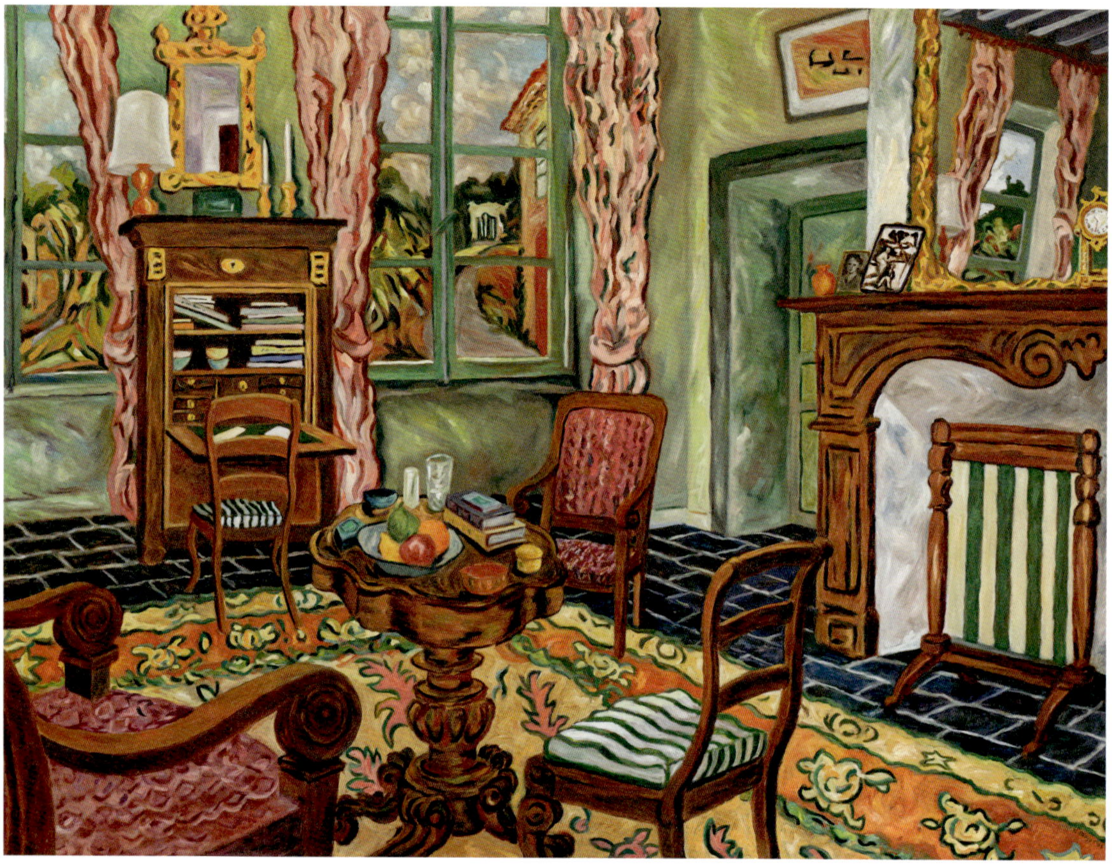

Le Salon de Mme Basseraux, 2001–25
Oil on linen
121.9 × 162.6 cm
48 × 64 in

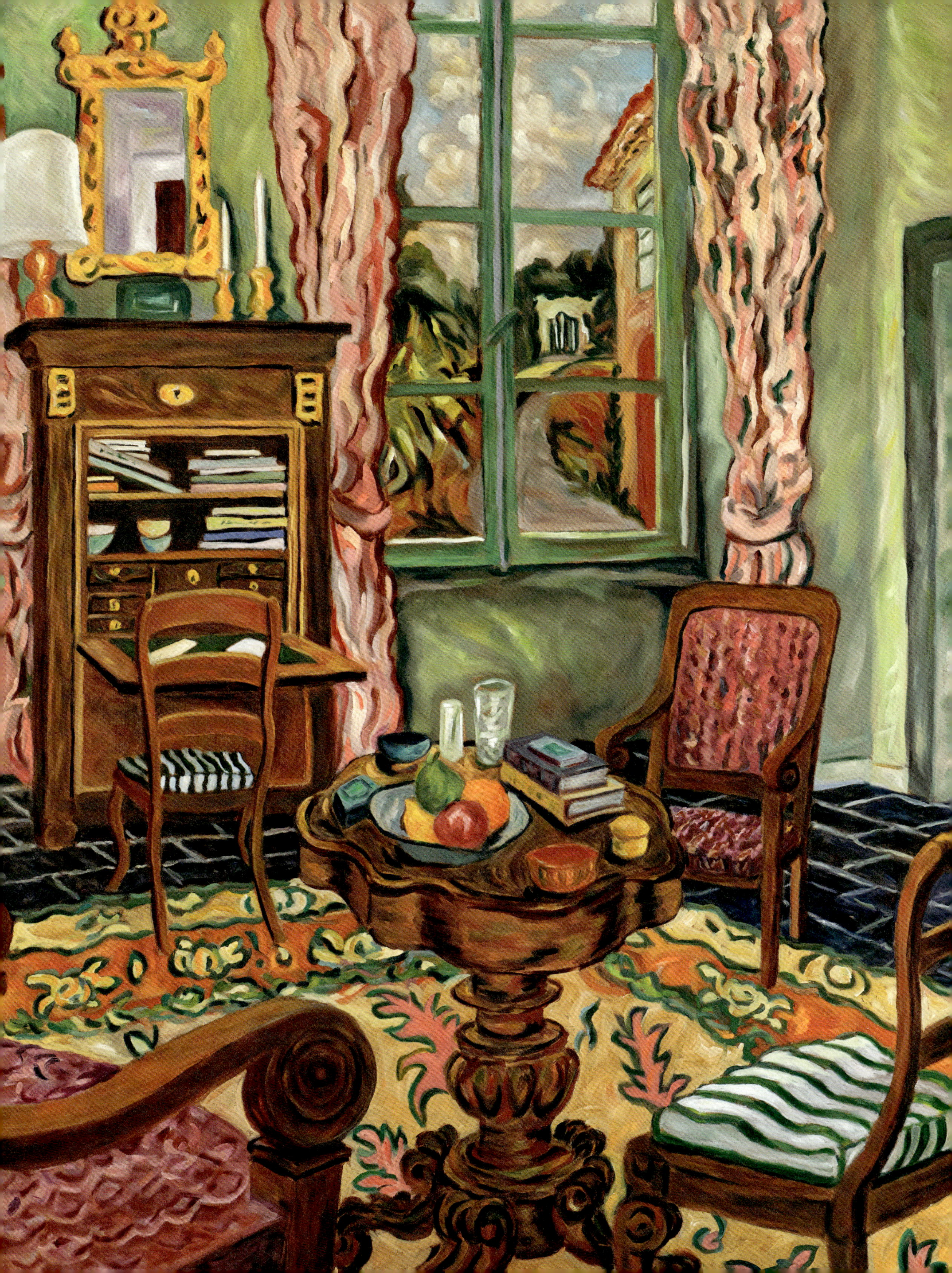

Le Secrétaire de Mme Basseraux, 2001–25
Oil on linen
162.6 × 121.9 cm
64 × 48 in

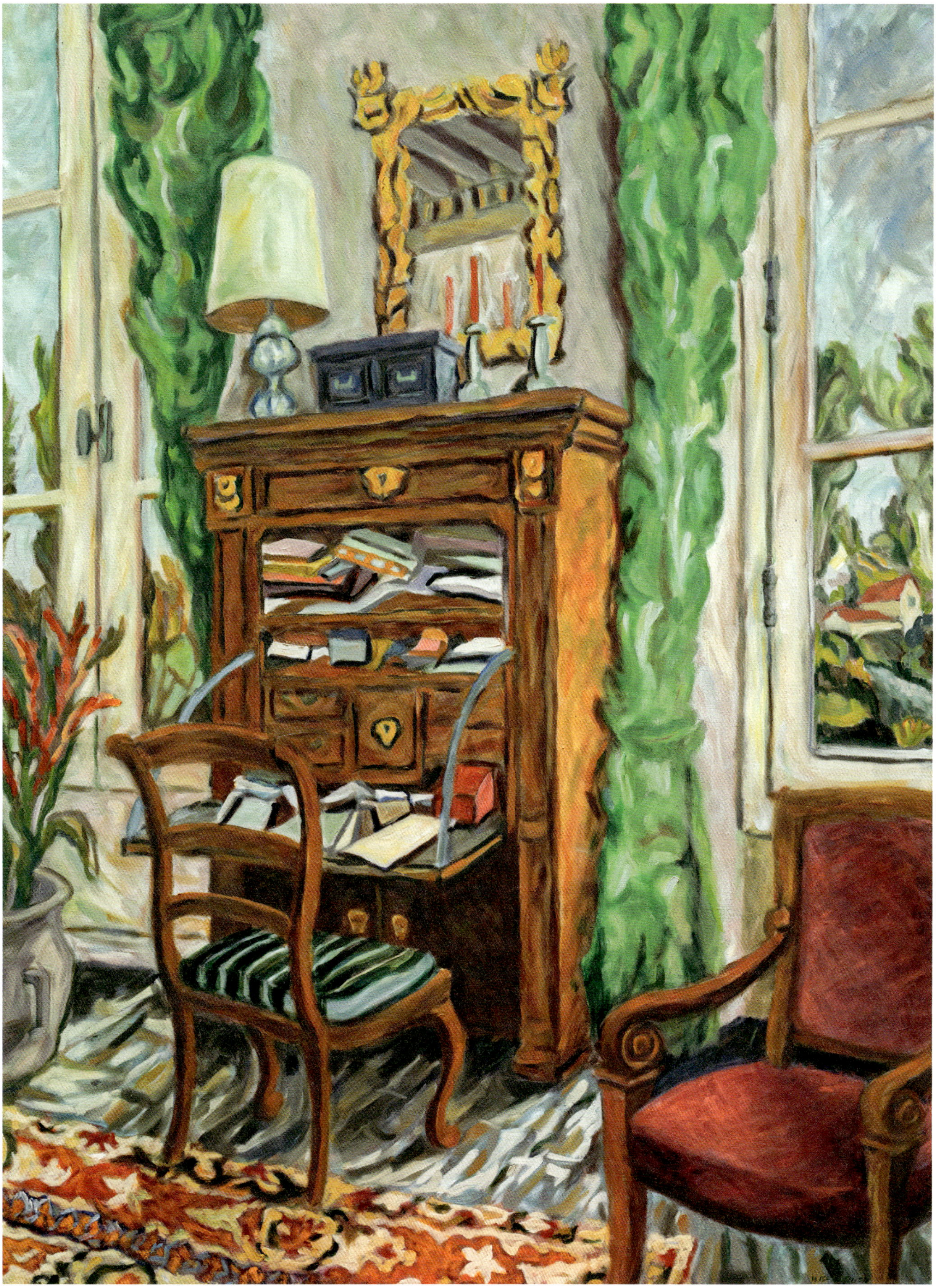

Magnetism, 2023
Oil on linen
76.2 × 101.6 cm
30 × 40 in

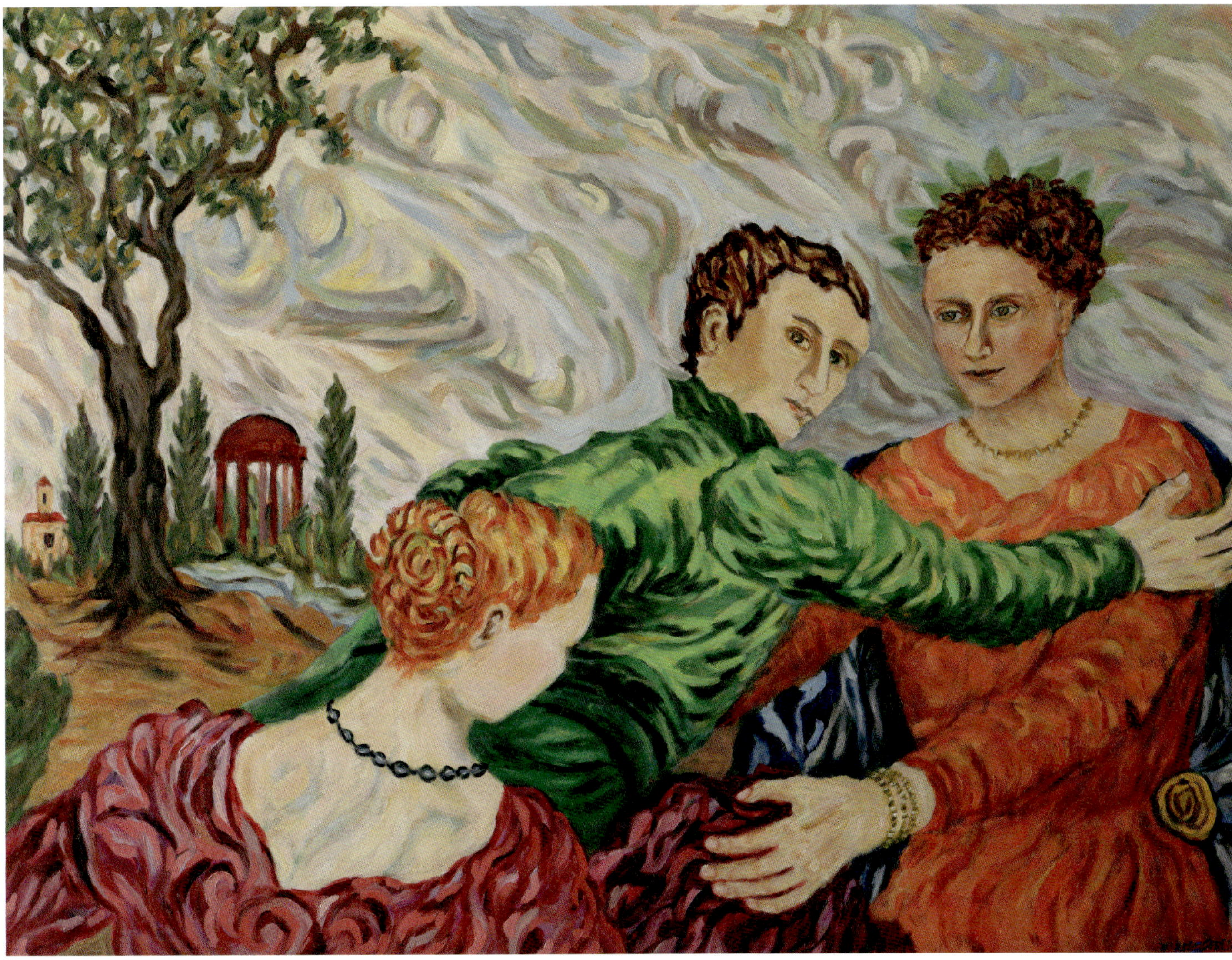

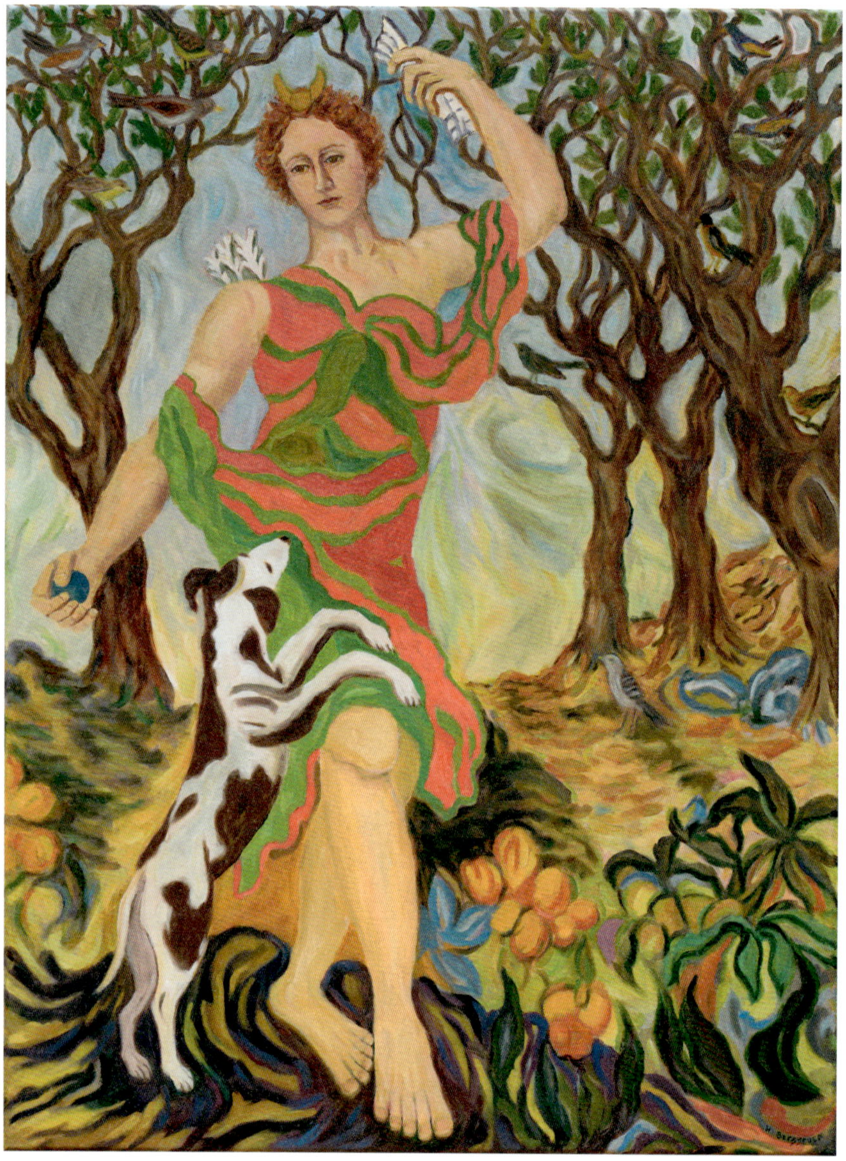

Diana, Goddess of the Hunt and of the Forest, 2025
Oil on linen
101.6 × 76.2 cm
40 × 30 in

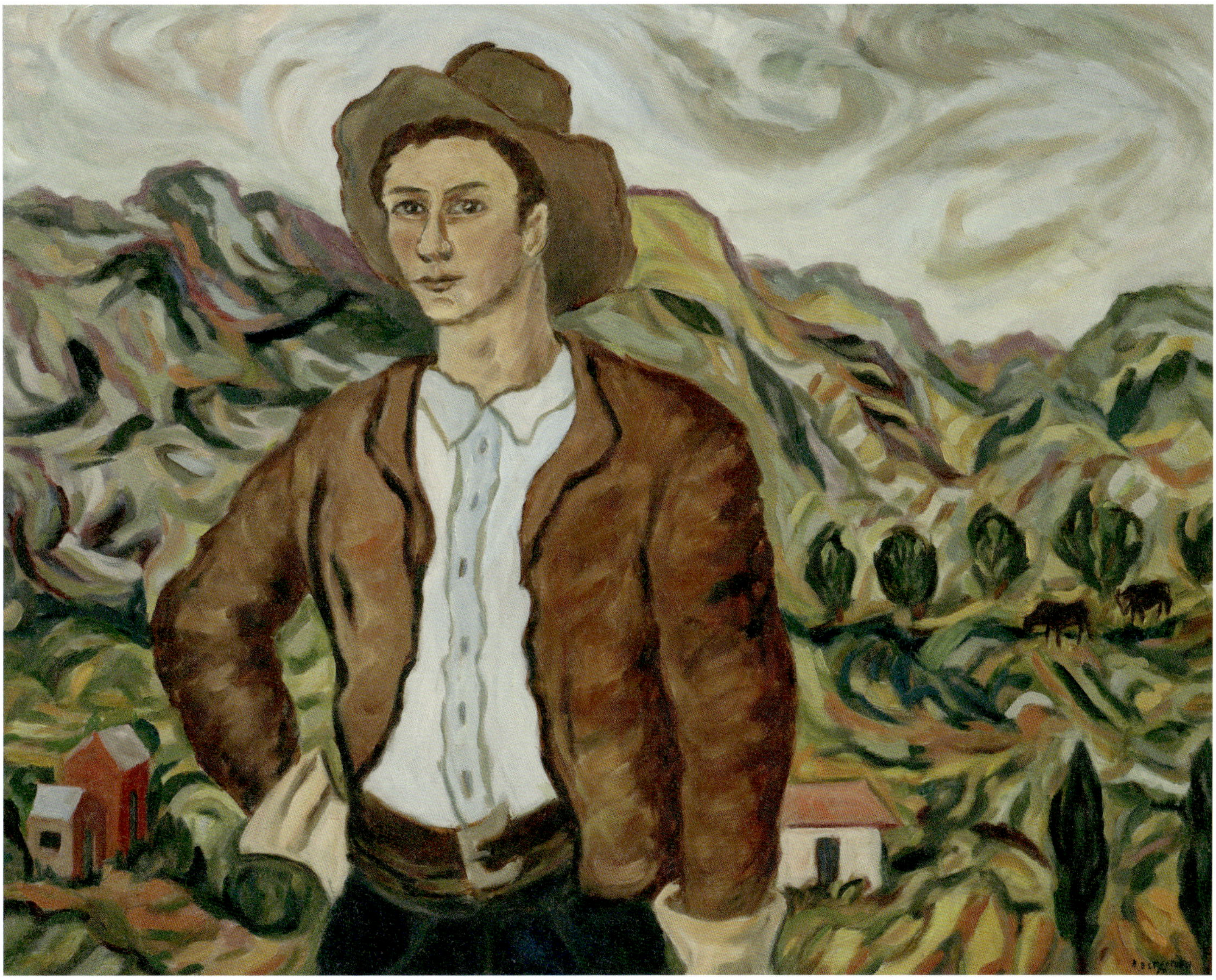

Cattle Ranch Hand, 2023
Oil on linen
55.9 × 71.1 cm
22 × 28 in

Hay Rolls, Road to St. Martin, 2025
Oil on linen
60.3 × 73 cm
23¾ × 28¾ in

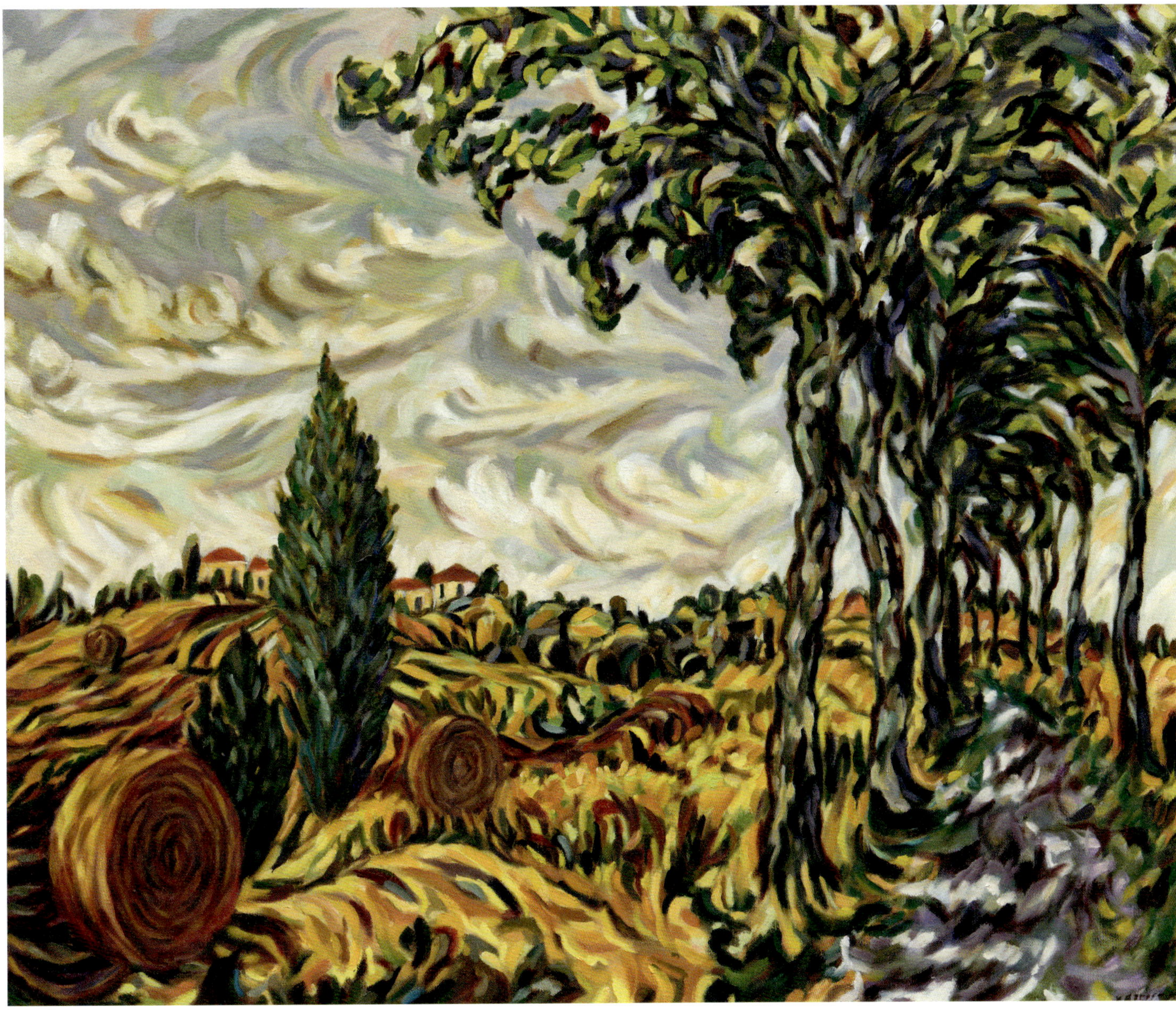

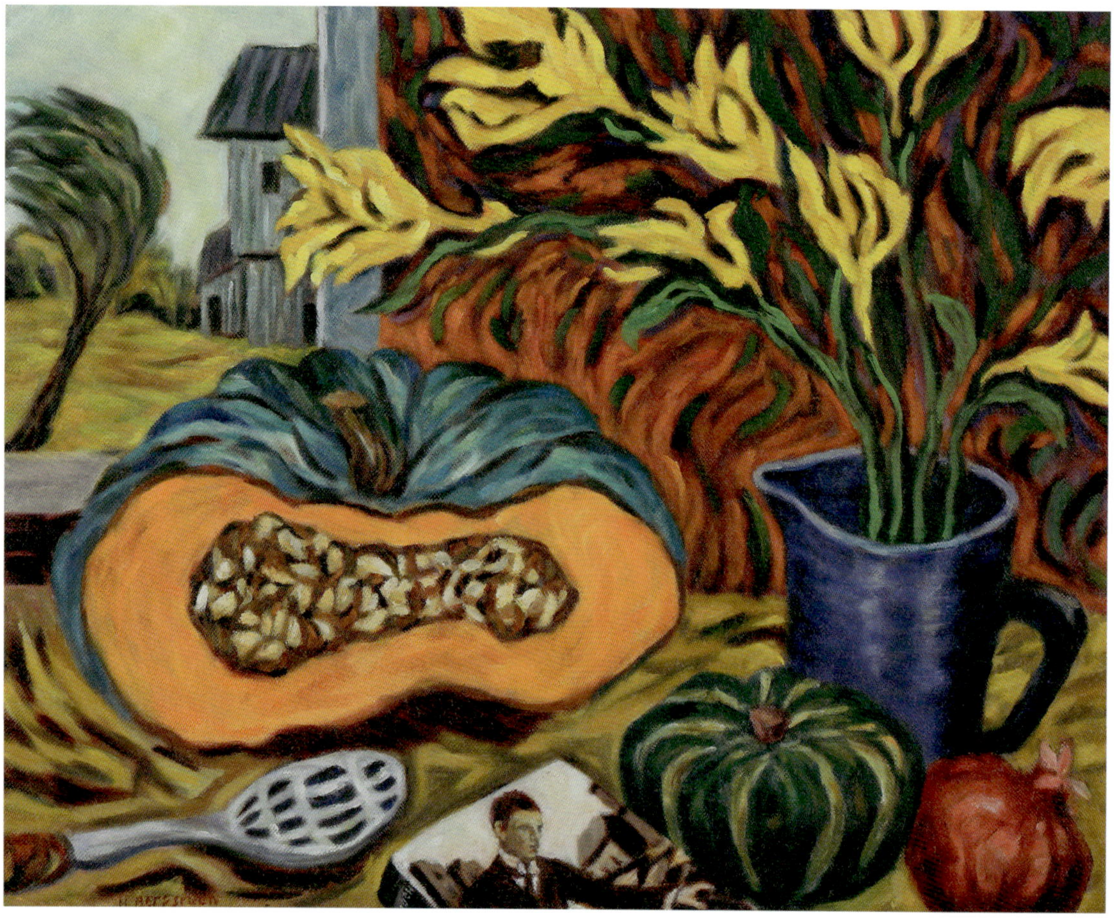

Still Life with Man on Balcony, 2013
Oil on linen
40.6 × 50.8 cm
16 × 20 in

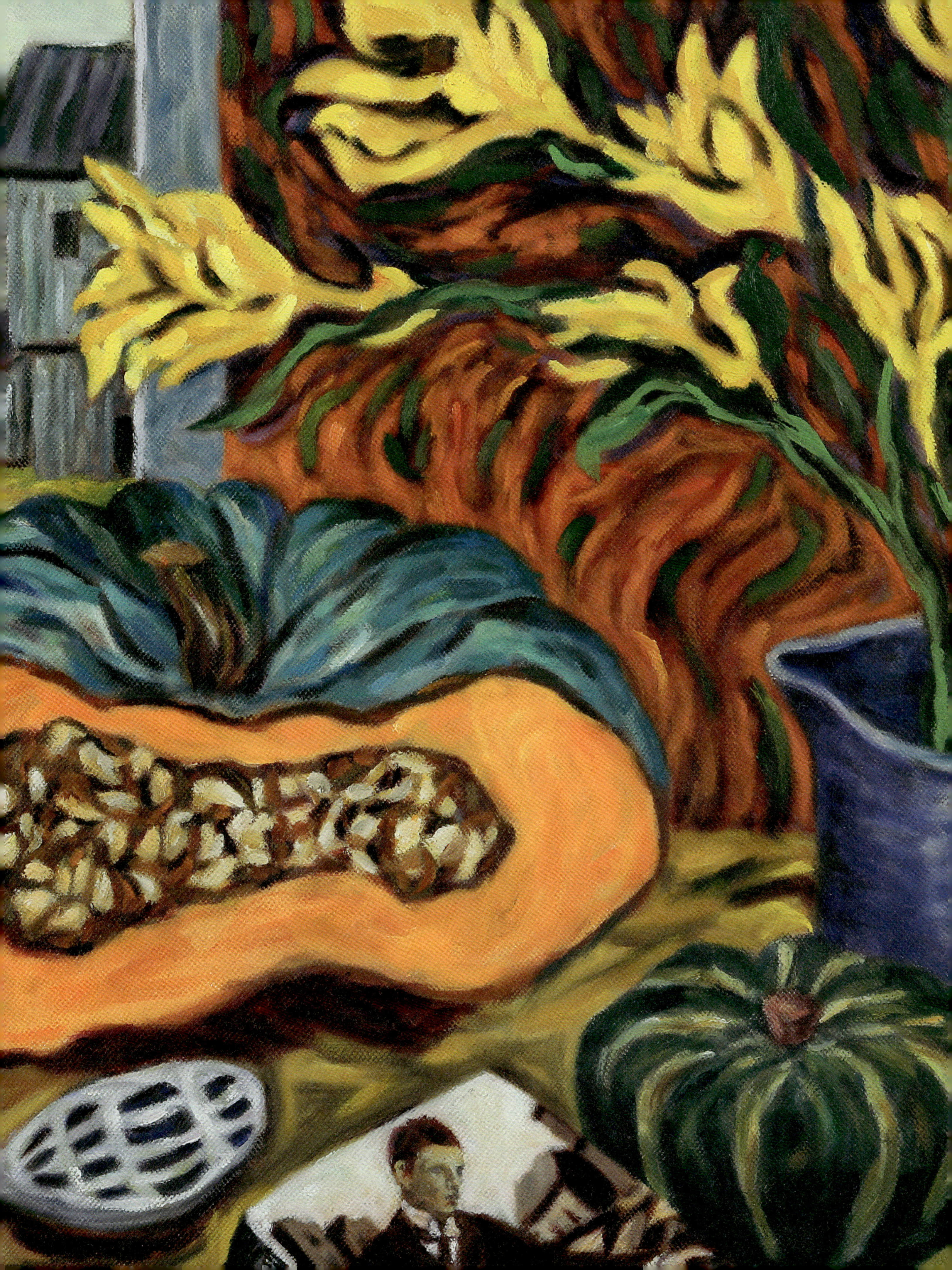

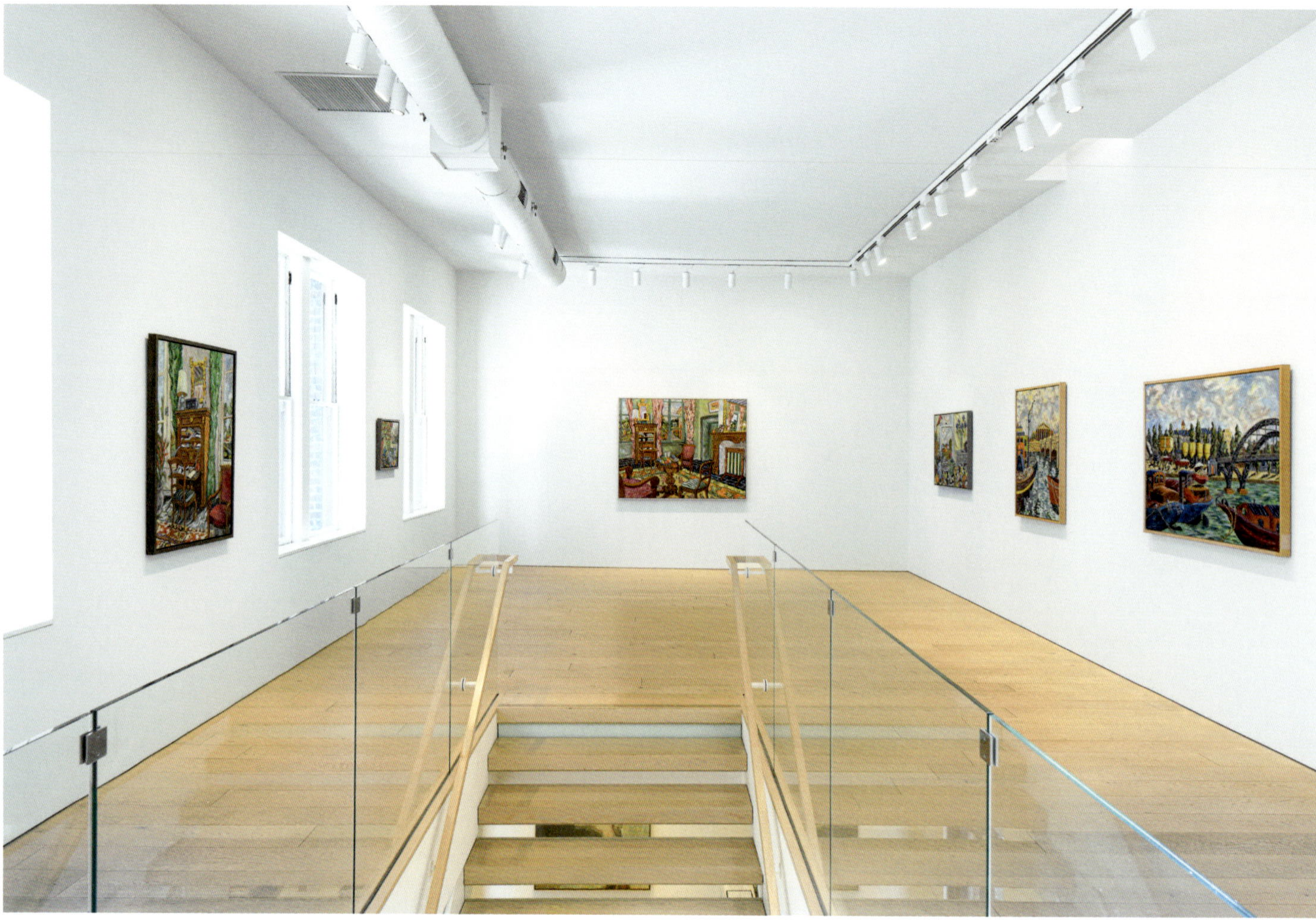

Exhibition views of *Helen Berggruen*
Berggruen Gallery, San Francisco
26 June – 14 August 2025

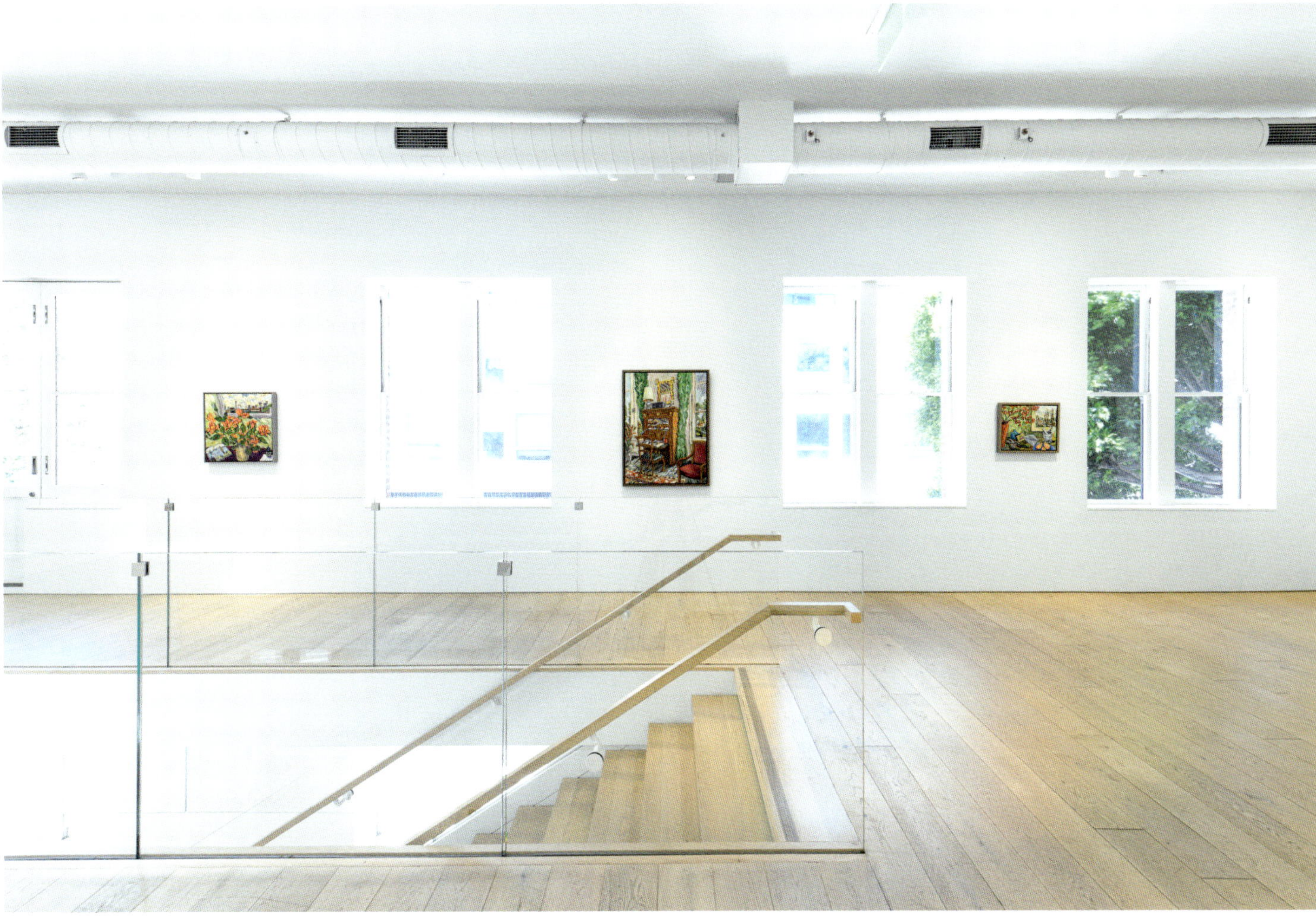

The Message, 2022
Oil on linen
55.9 × 71.1 cm
22 × 28 in

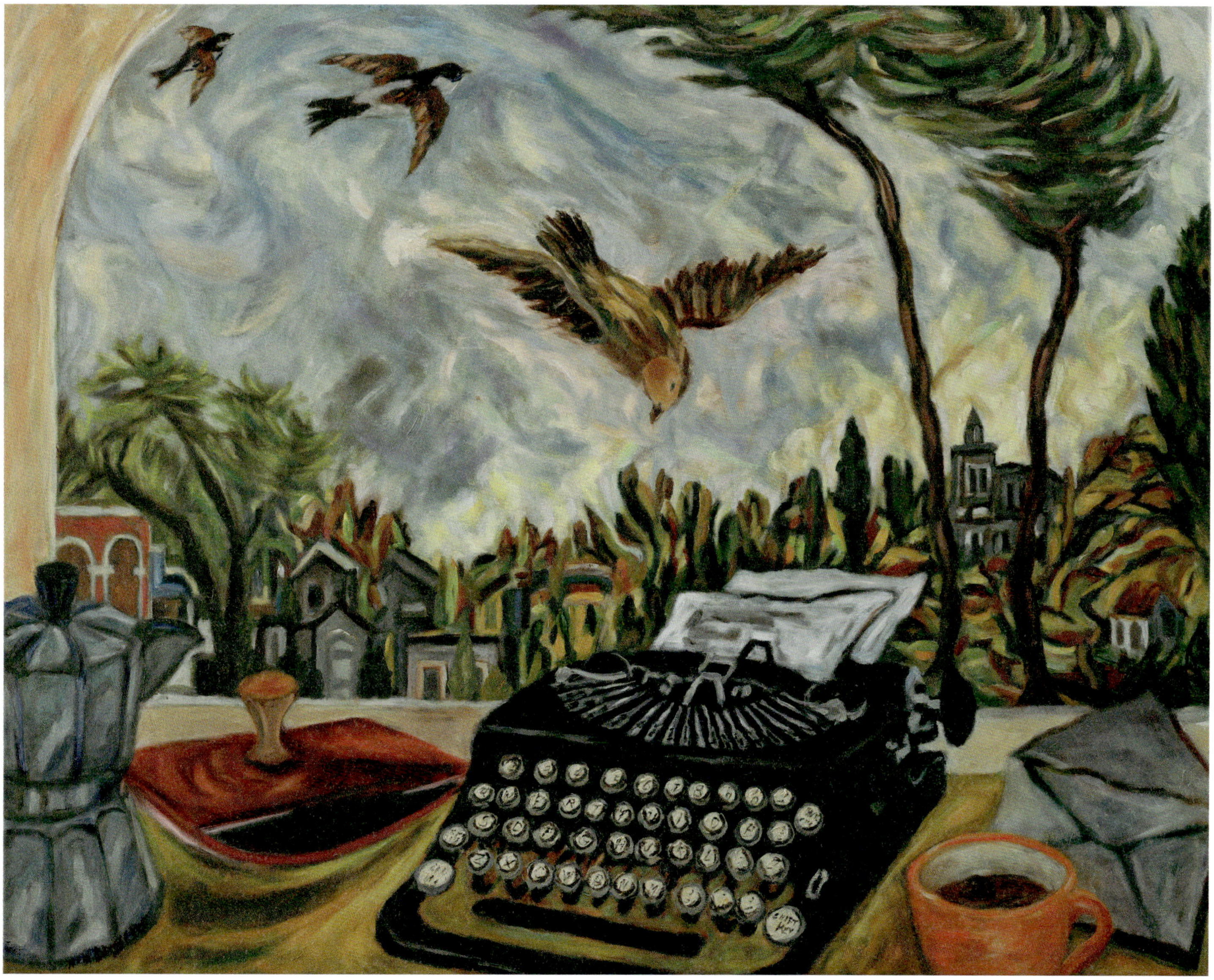

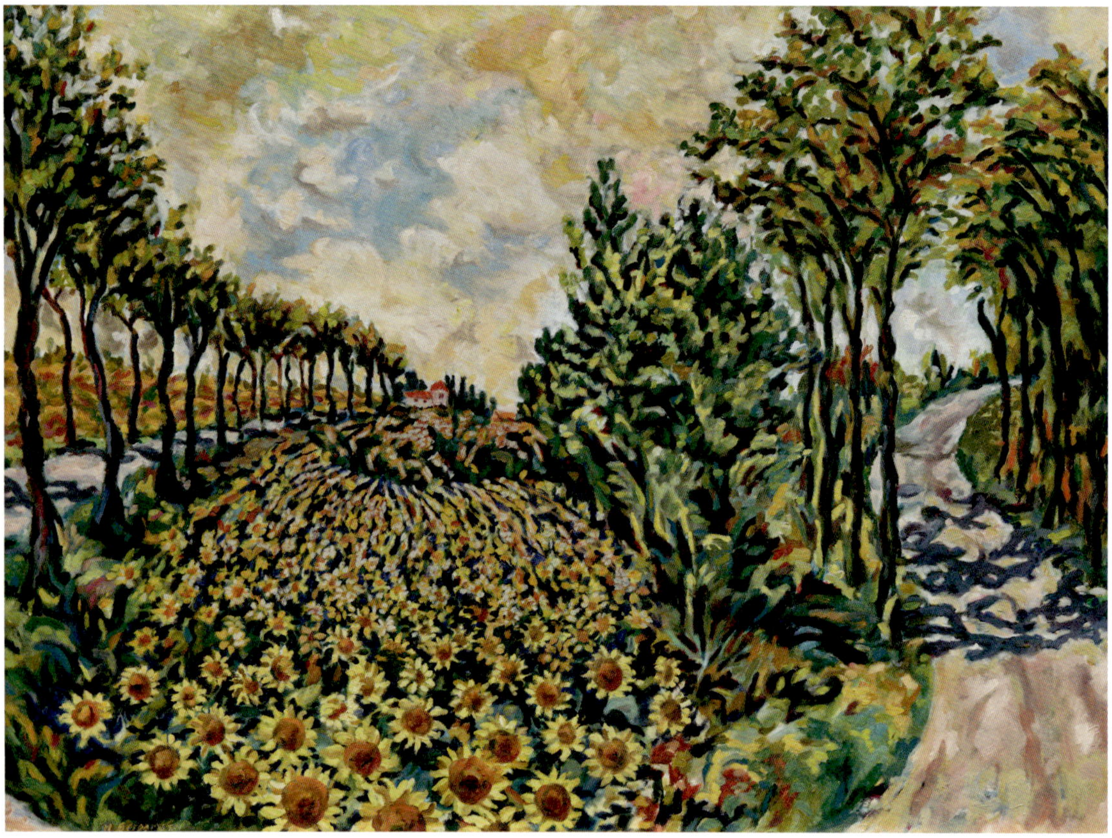

Virage, 2002
Oil on linen
55.9 × 71.1 cm
22 × 28 in

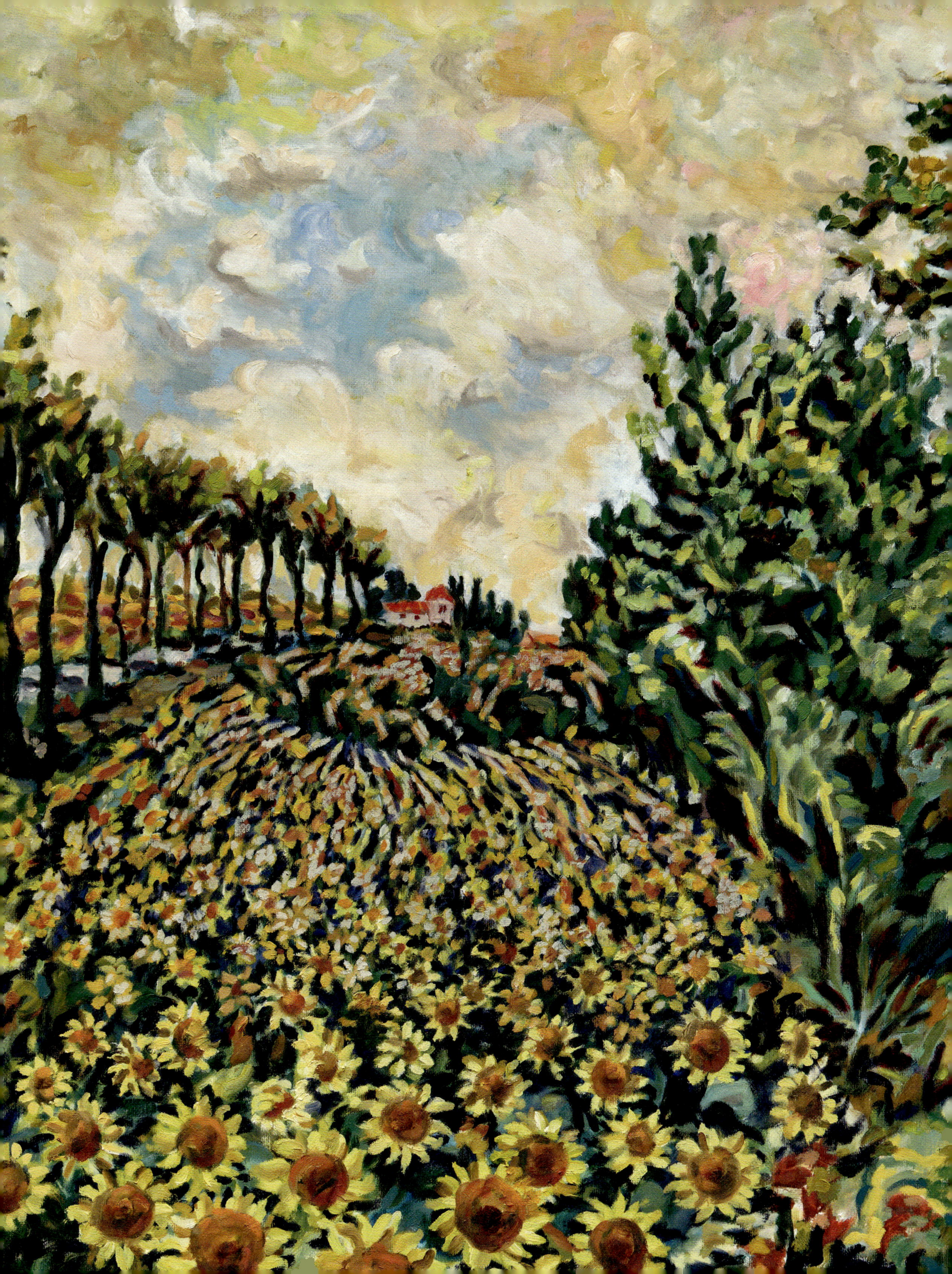

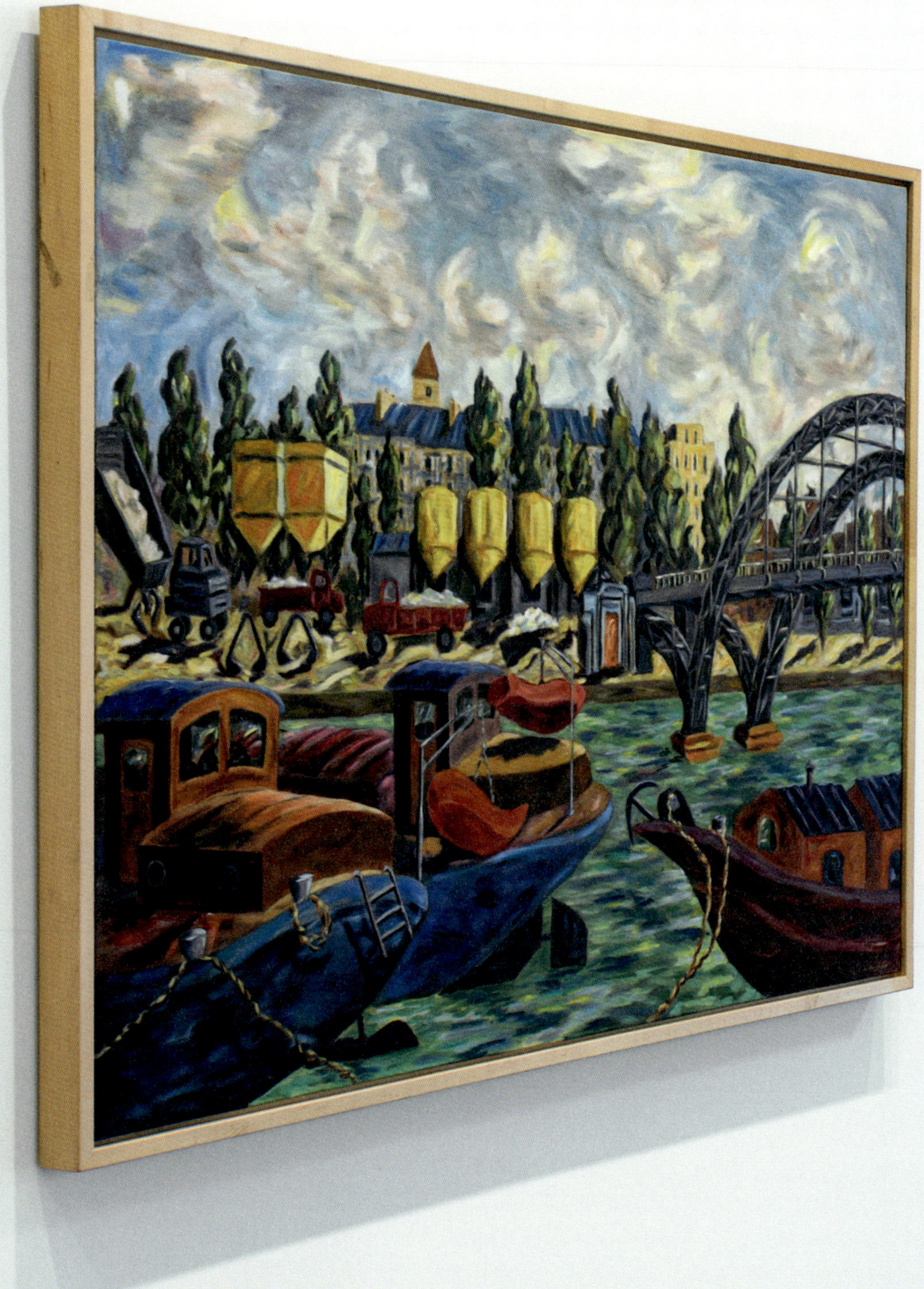

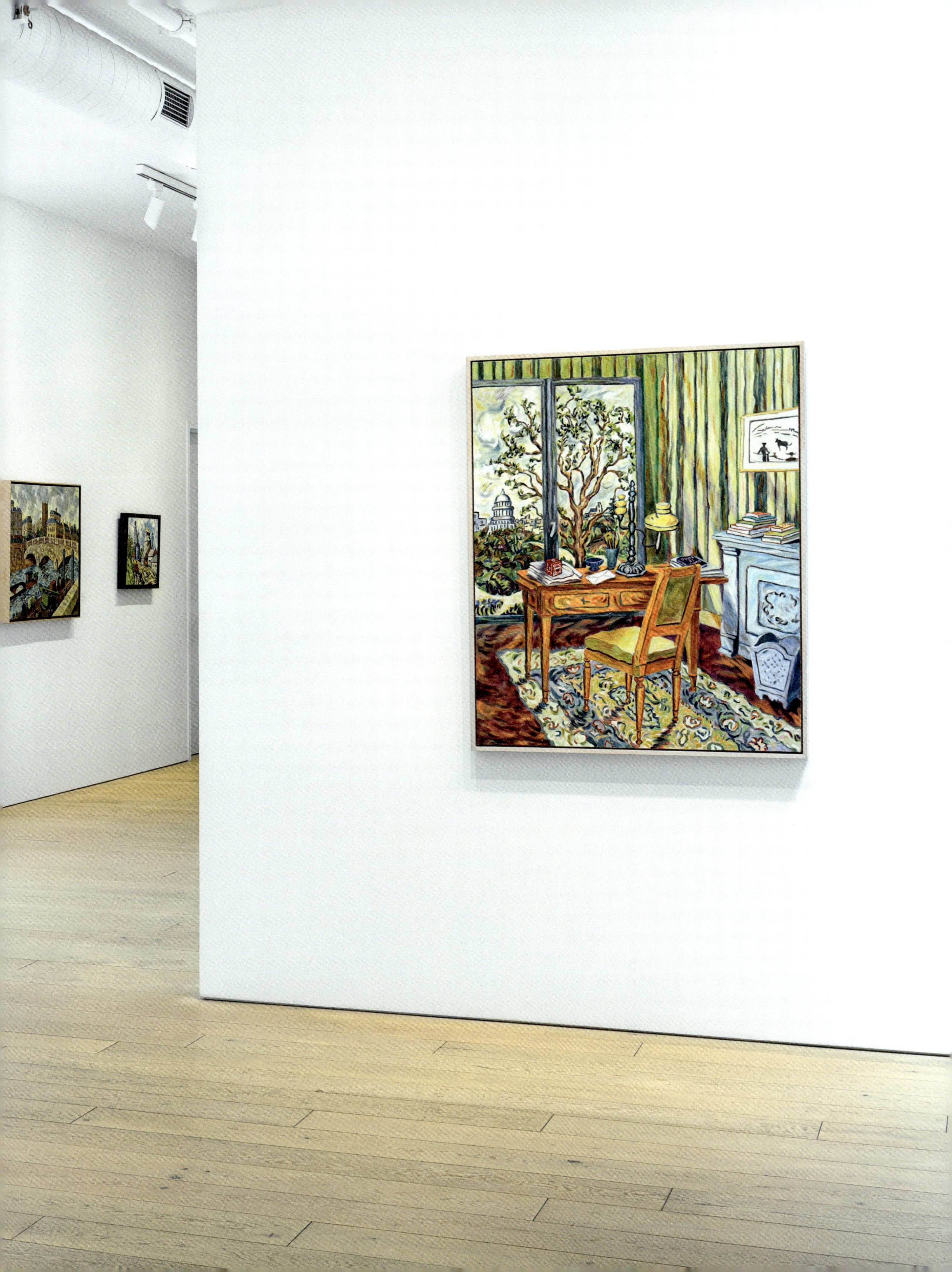

Yellow Tractor, Paris Storefront, 1994–2025
Oil on linen
68.6 × 83.8 cm
27 × 33 in

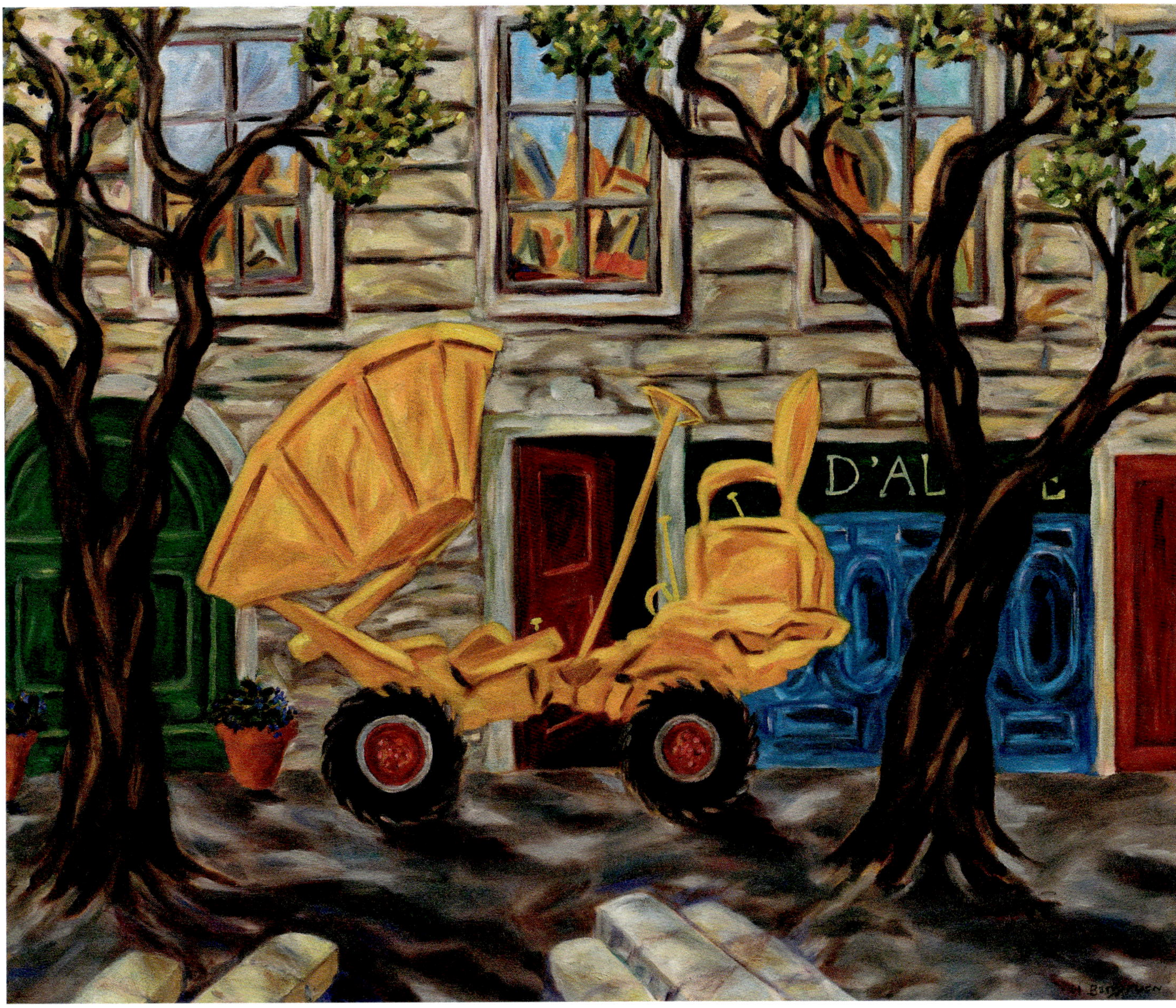

Street Work, Blvd. Richard Lemoine, 1994–2025
Oil on linen
54.6 × 64.7 cm
21½ × 25½ in

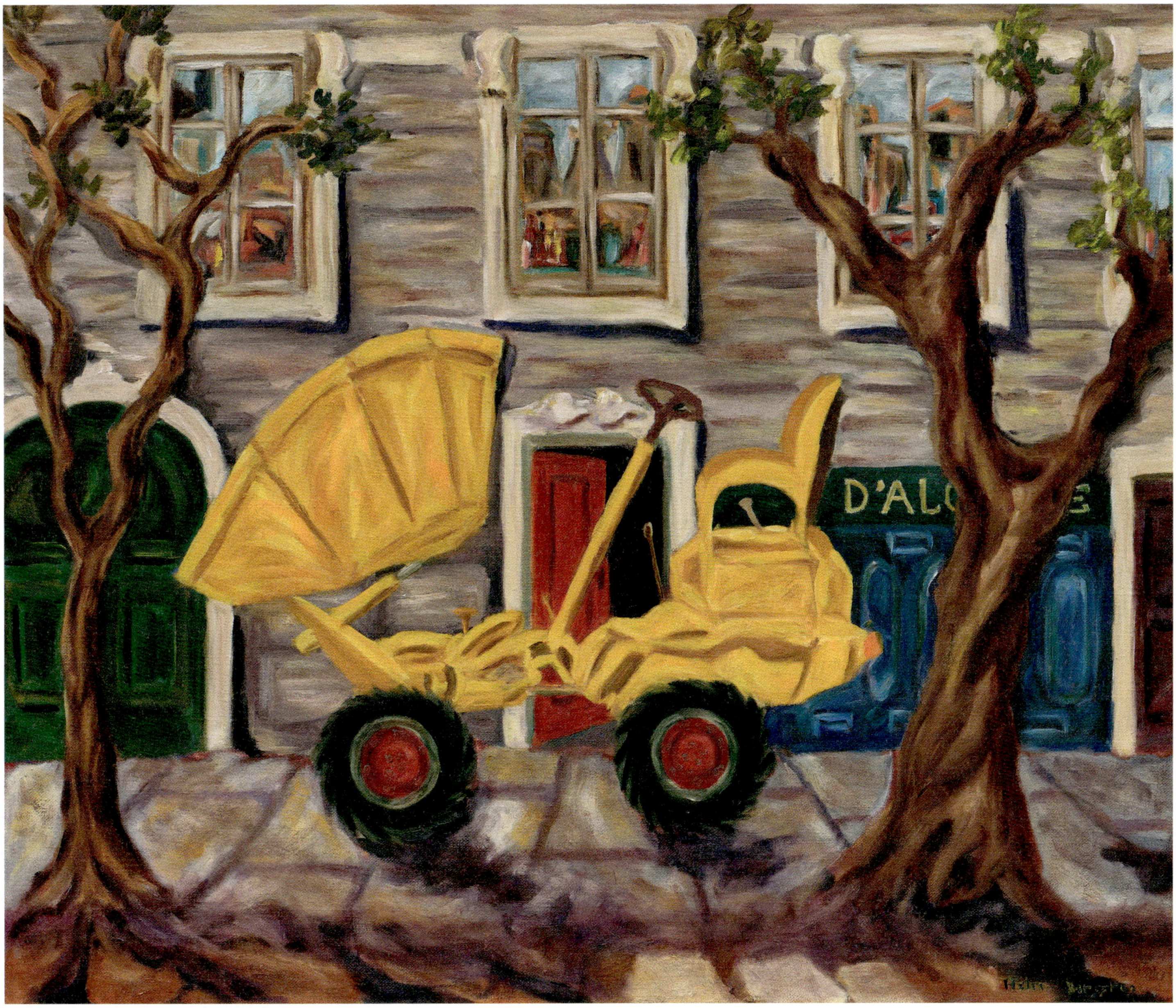
D'AL

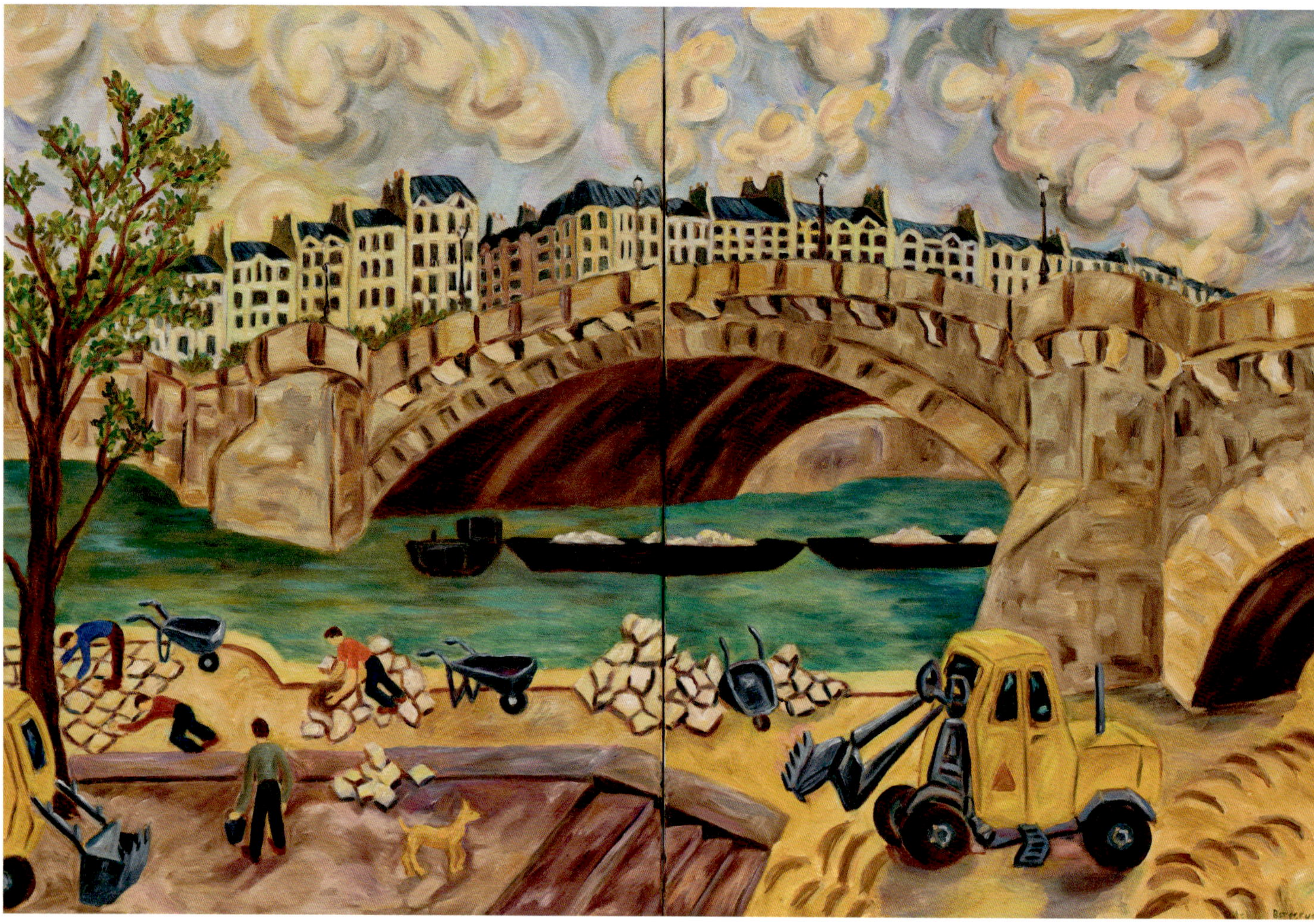

Stonework, Quai Conti (diptych), 1994–2025
Oil on linen
73 cm × 108 cm
28¾ × 42½ in

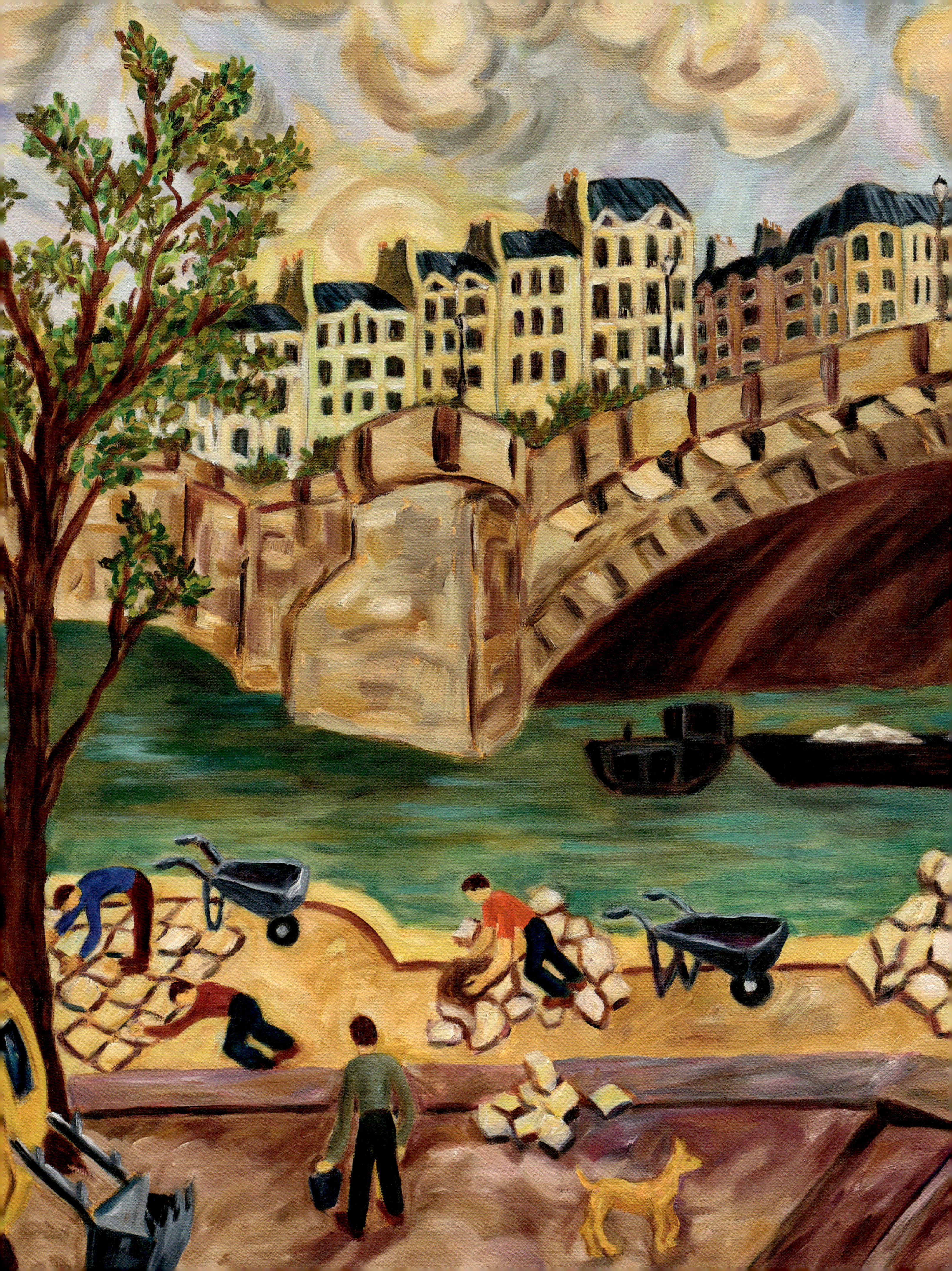

Appoggiatura, 2025
Oil on linen
55.9 × 71.1 cm
22 × 28 in

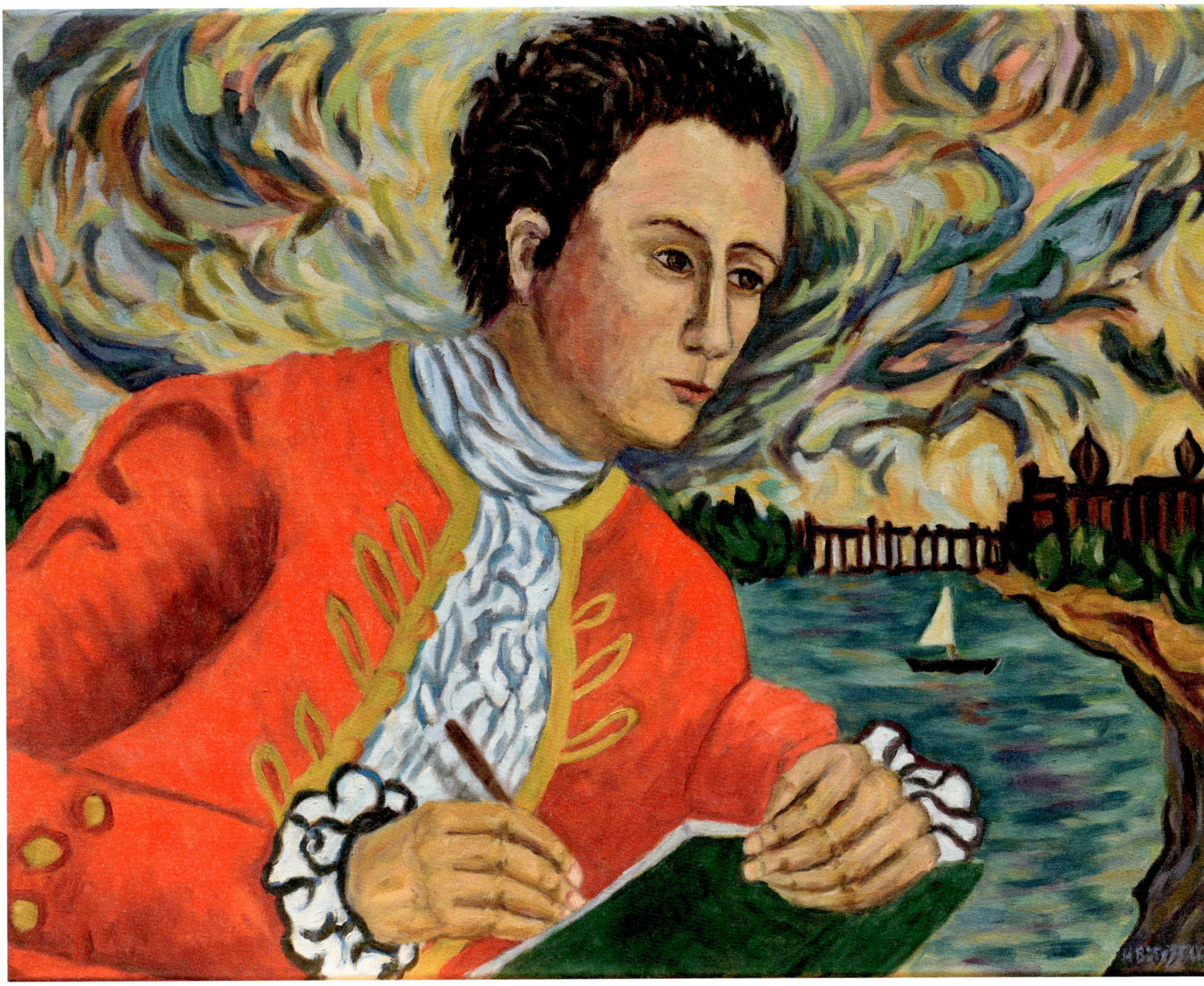

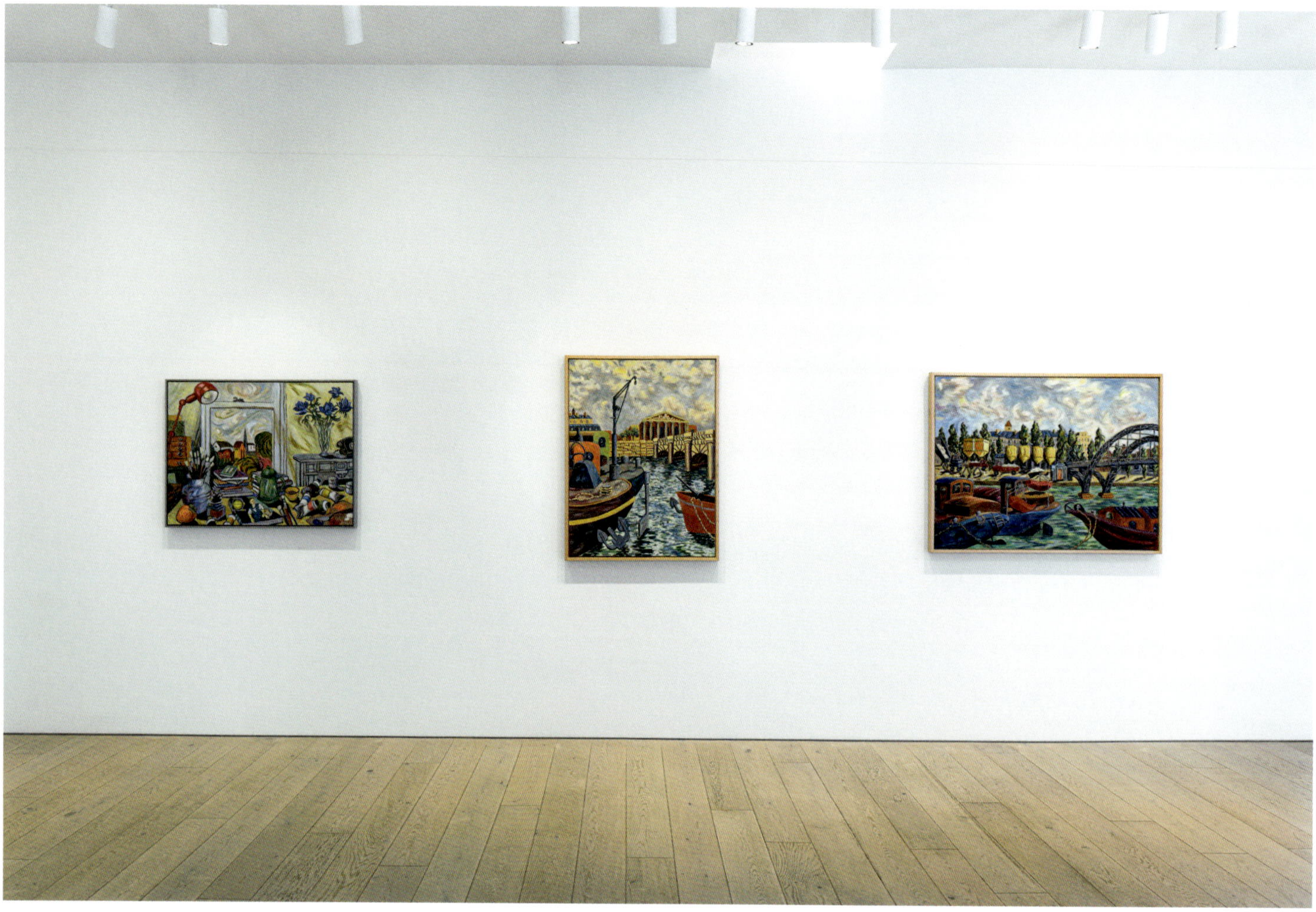

Exhibition views of *Helen Berggruen*
Berggruen Gallery, San Francisco
26 June – 14 August 2025

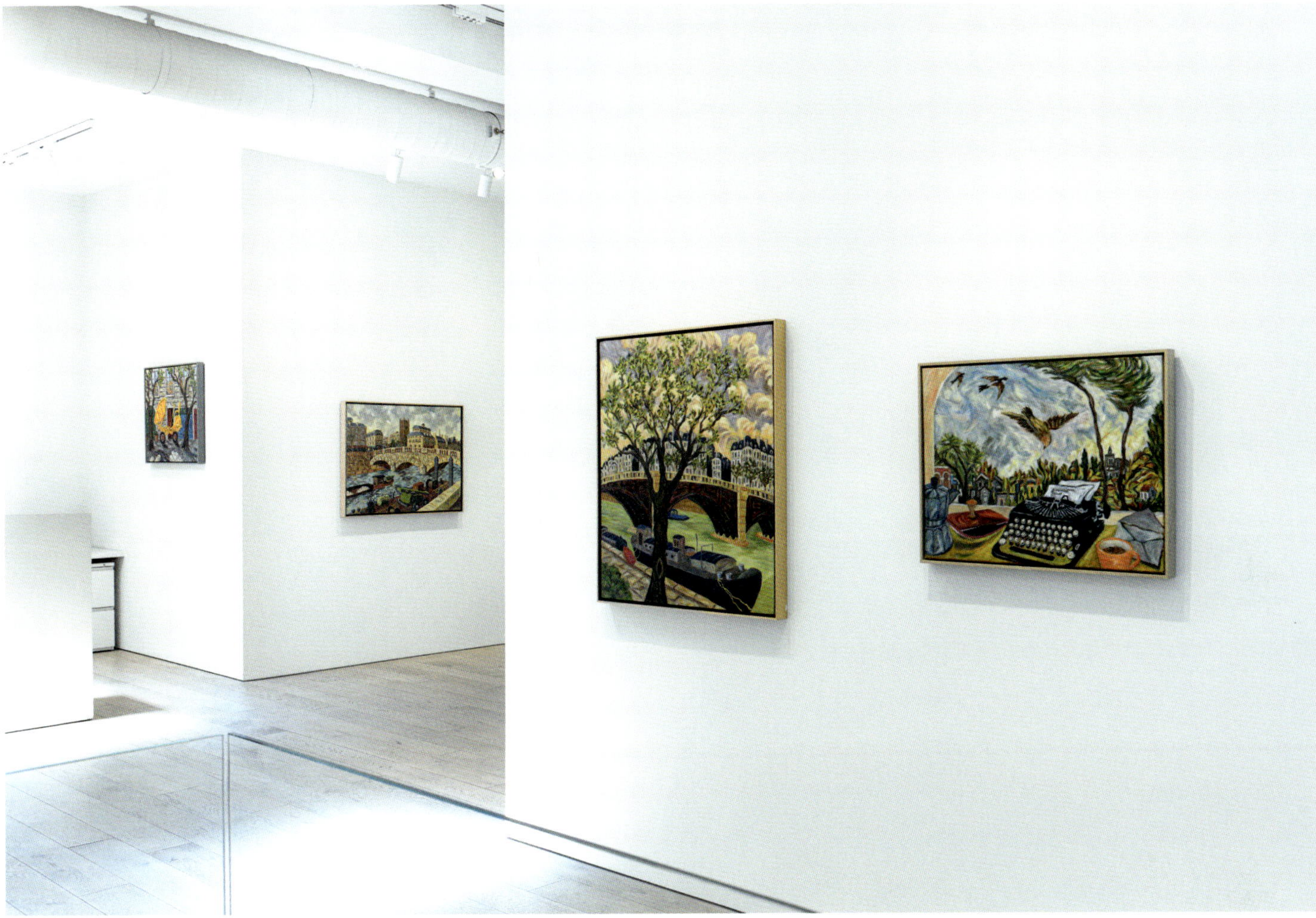

Paris Cement Mixers, 2025
Oil on canvas
91.4 × 121.9 cm
36 × 48 in

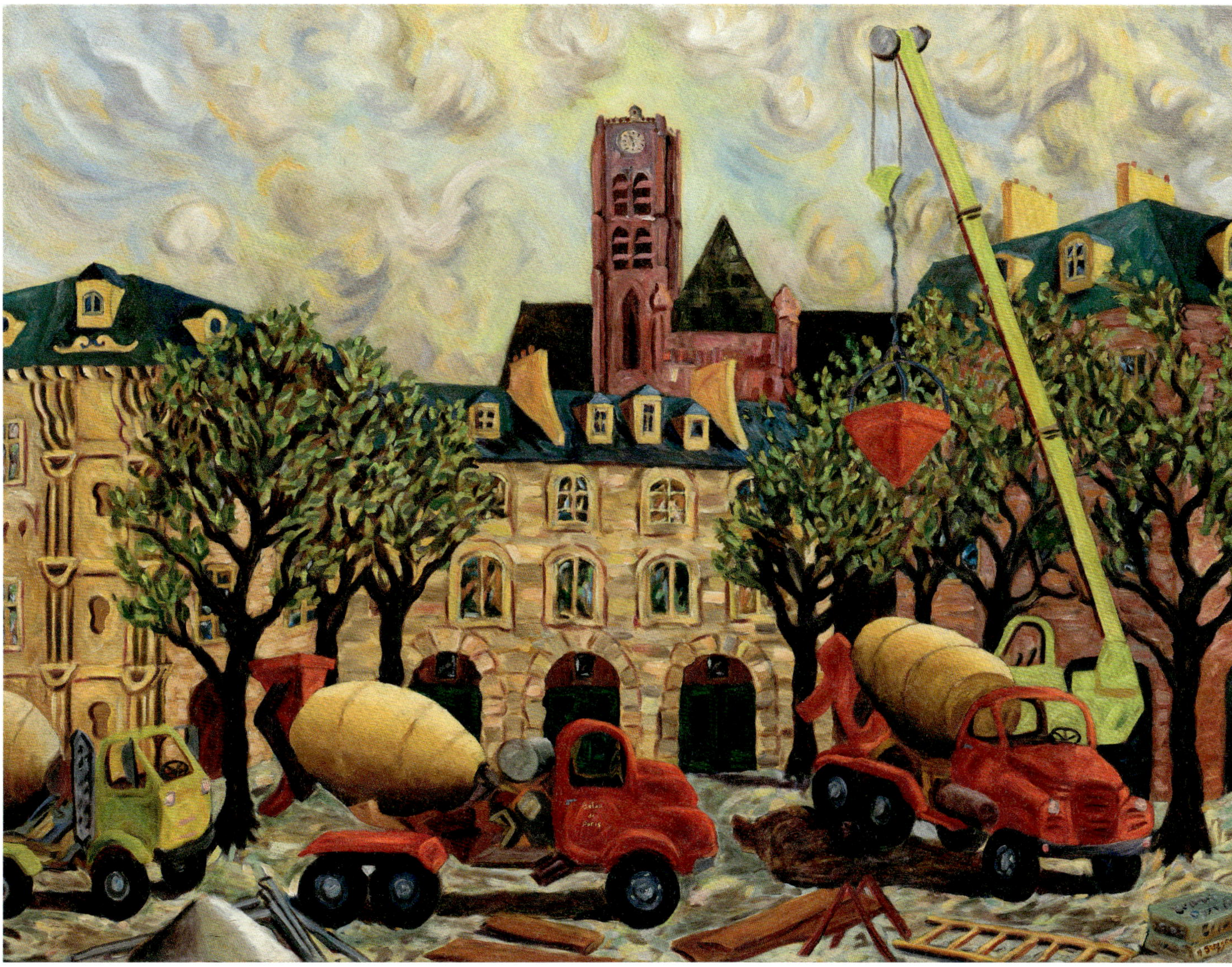

Port of Call, 2025
Oil on canvas
76.2 × 101.6 cm
30 × 40 in

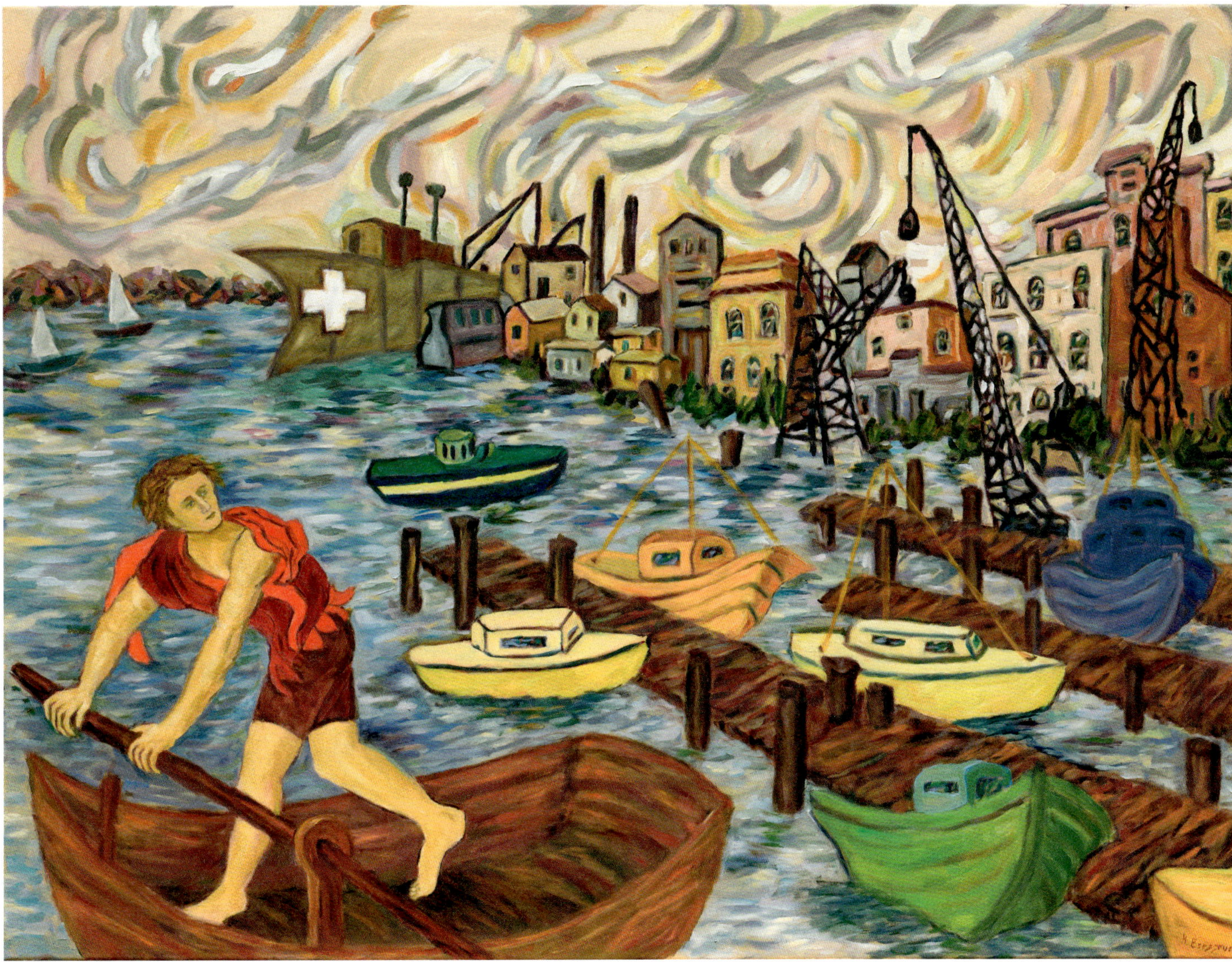

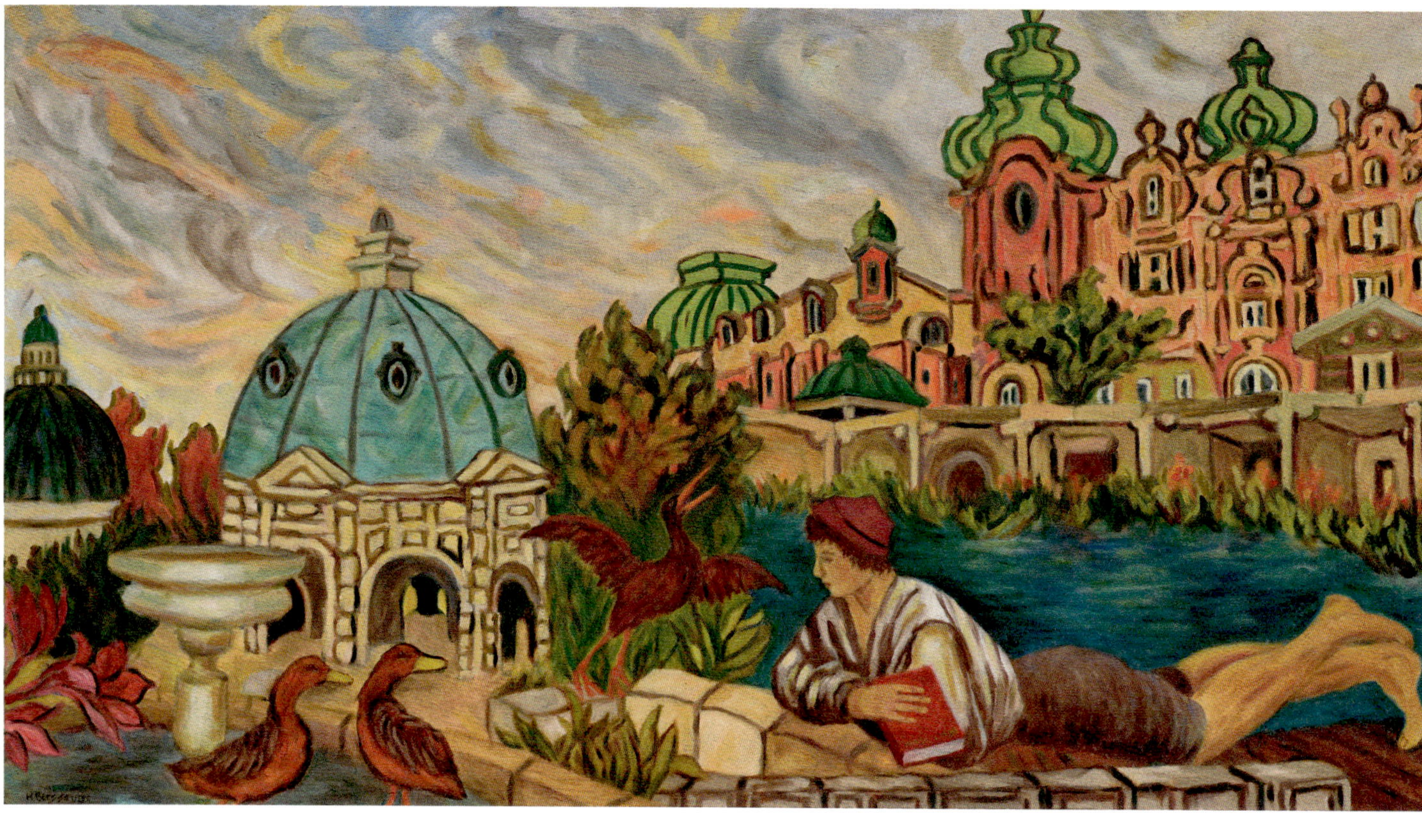

Song of the Water Rail, 2025
Oil on linen
61 × 111.8 cm
24 × 44 in

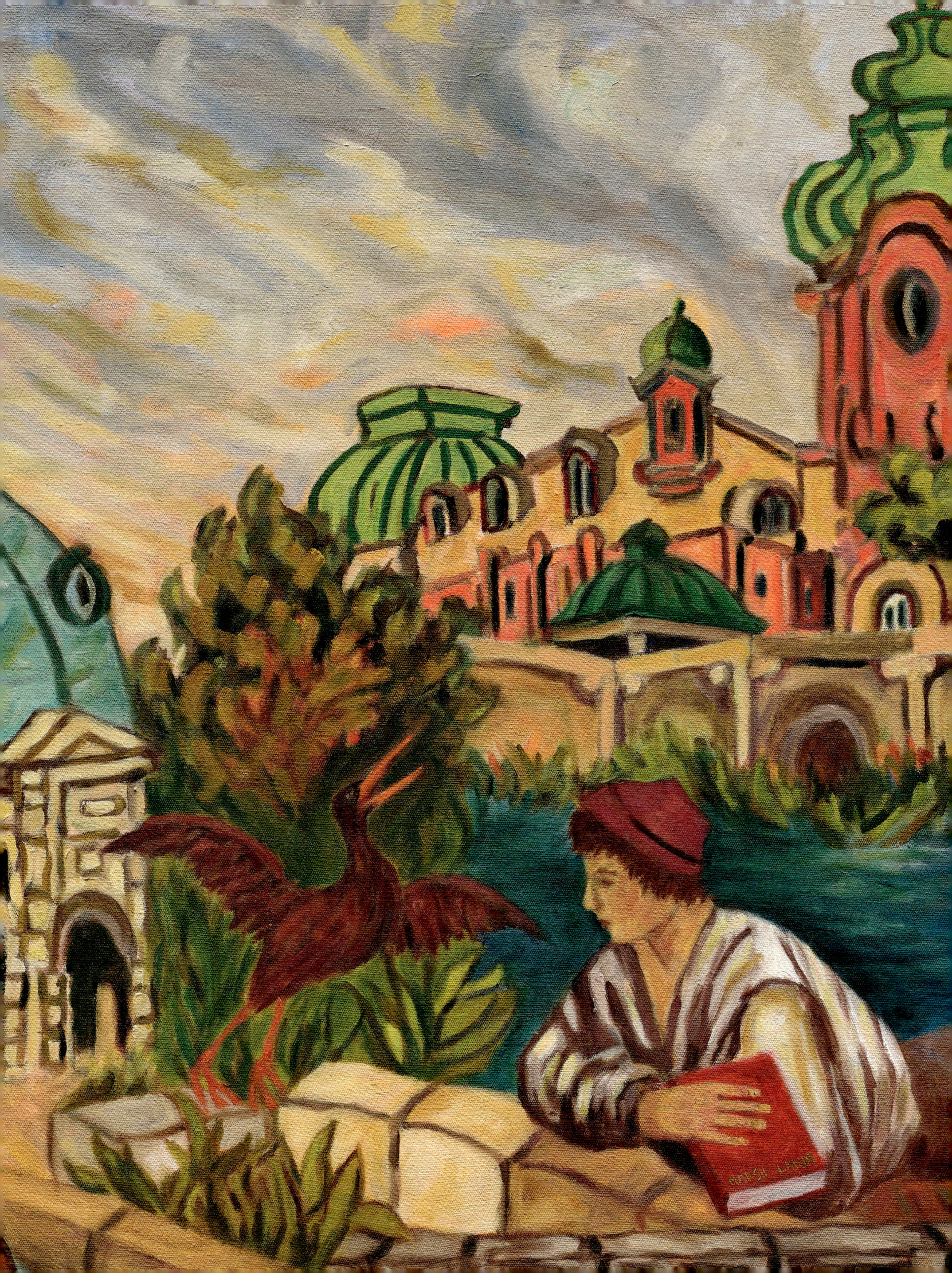

Machinist's Apprentice, 2024
Oil on linen
101.6 × 76.2 cm
40 × 30 in

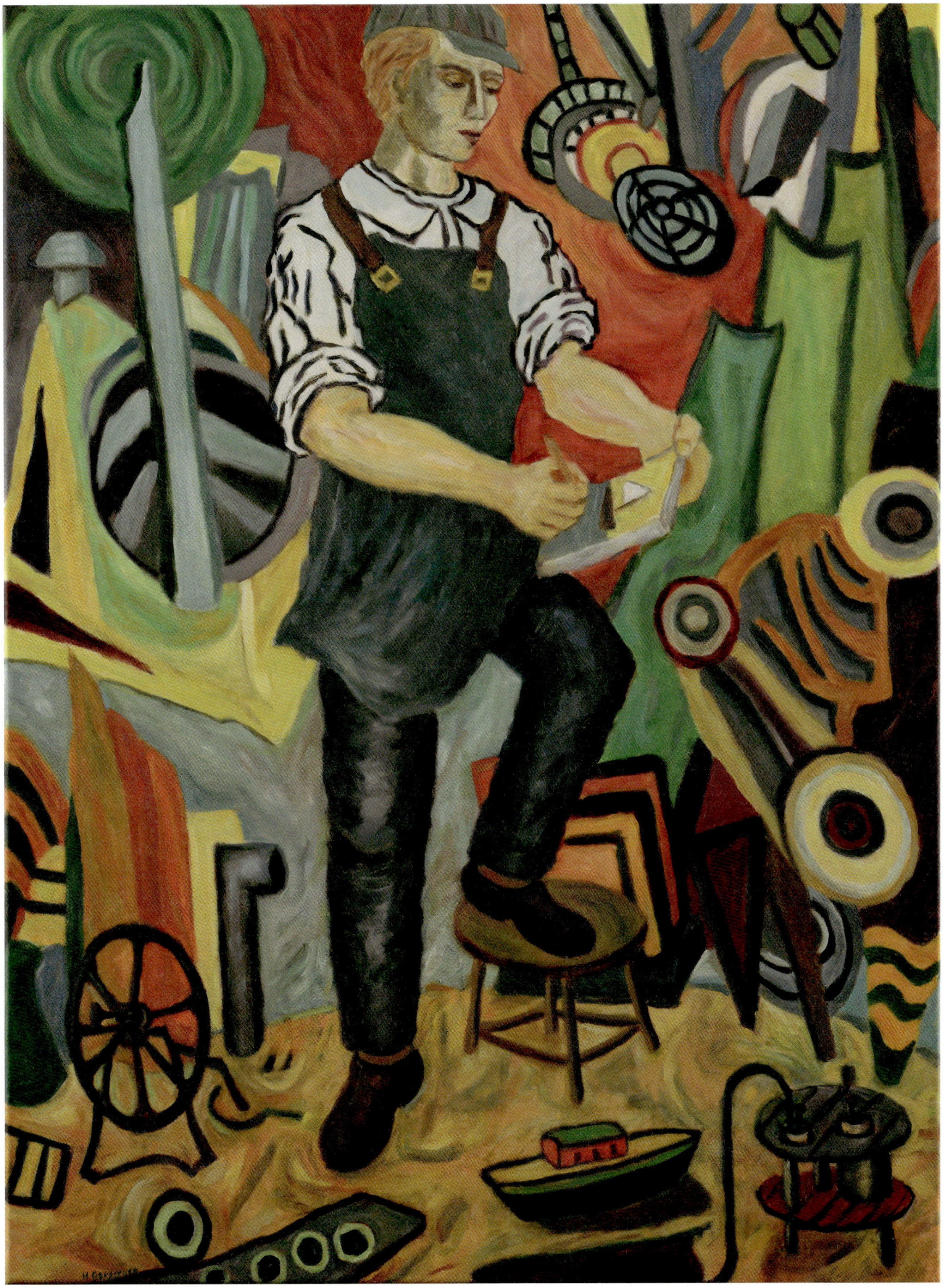

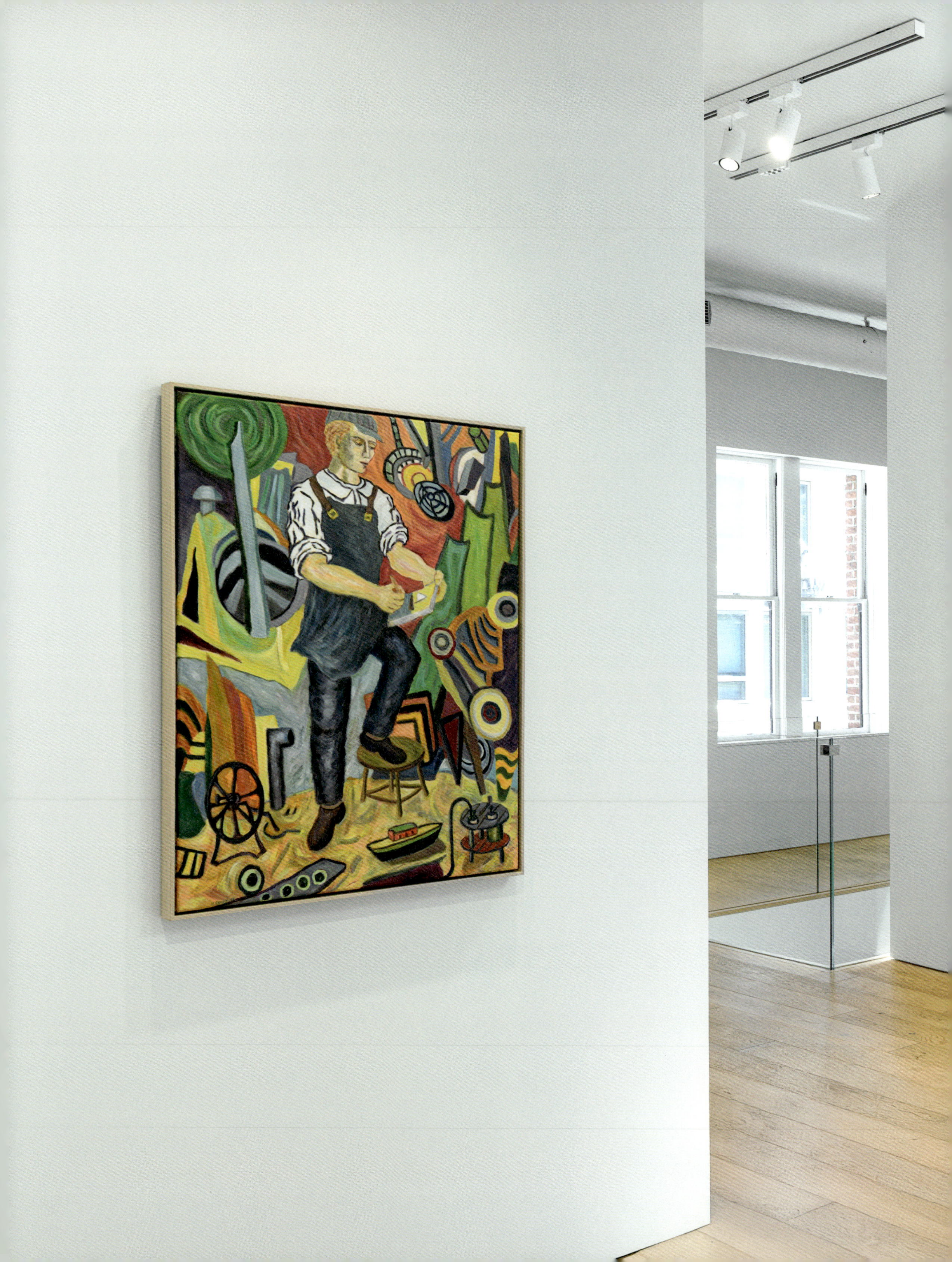

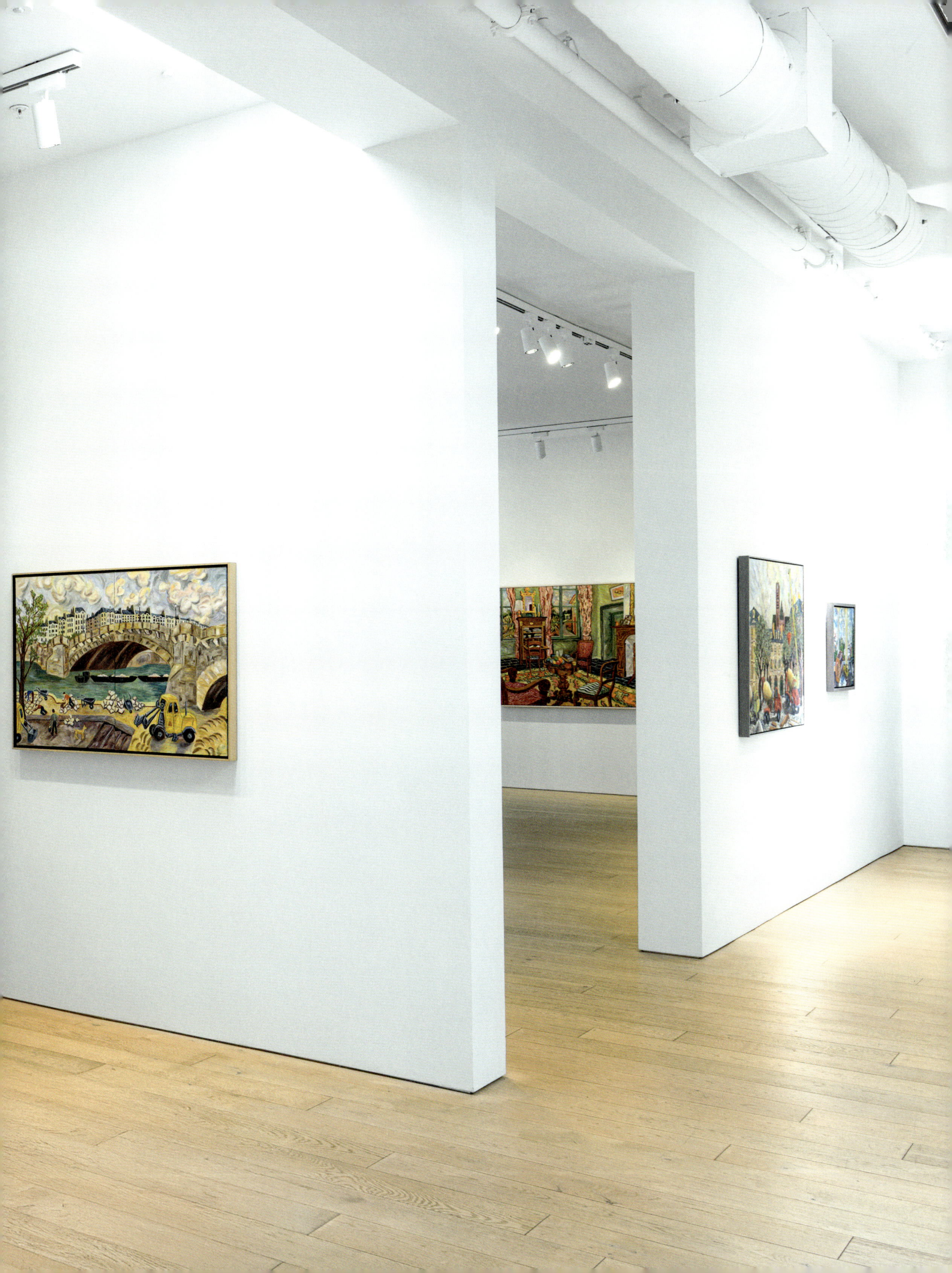

Pont de la Tournelle, 1995–2025
Oil on linen
94 × 81.3 cm
37 × 32 in

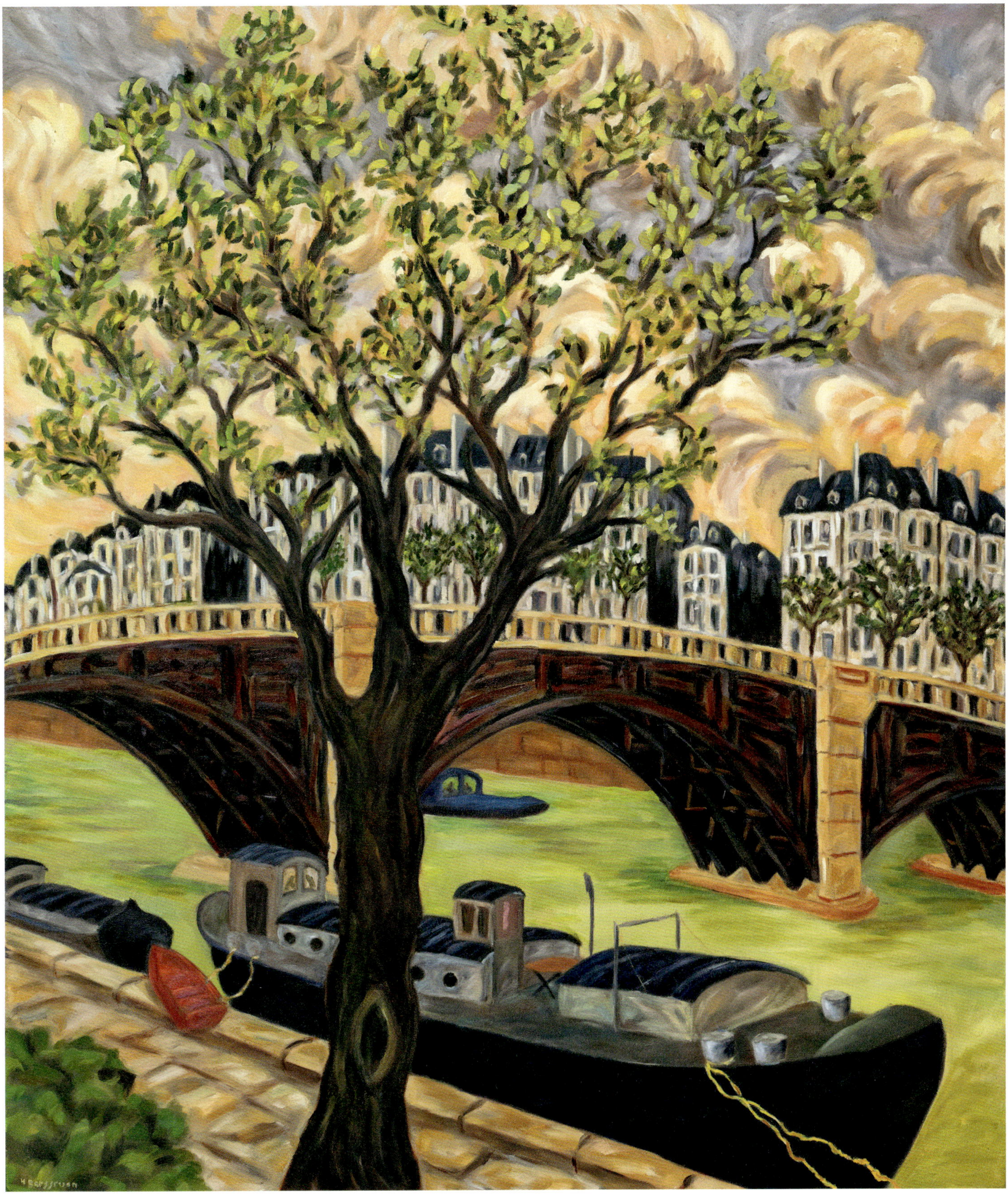

Sunflowers & Figure in Front of Mirror, 2020
Oil on linen
61 × 61 cm
24 × 24 in

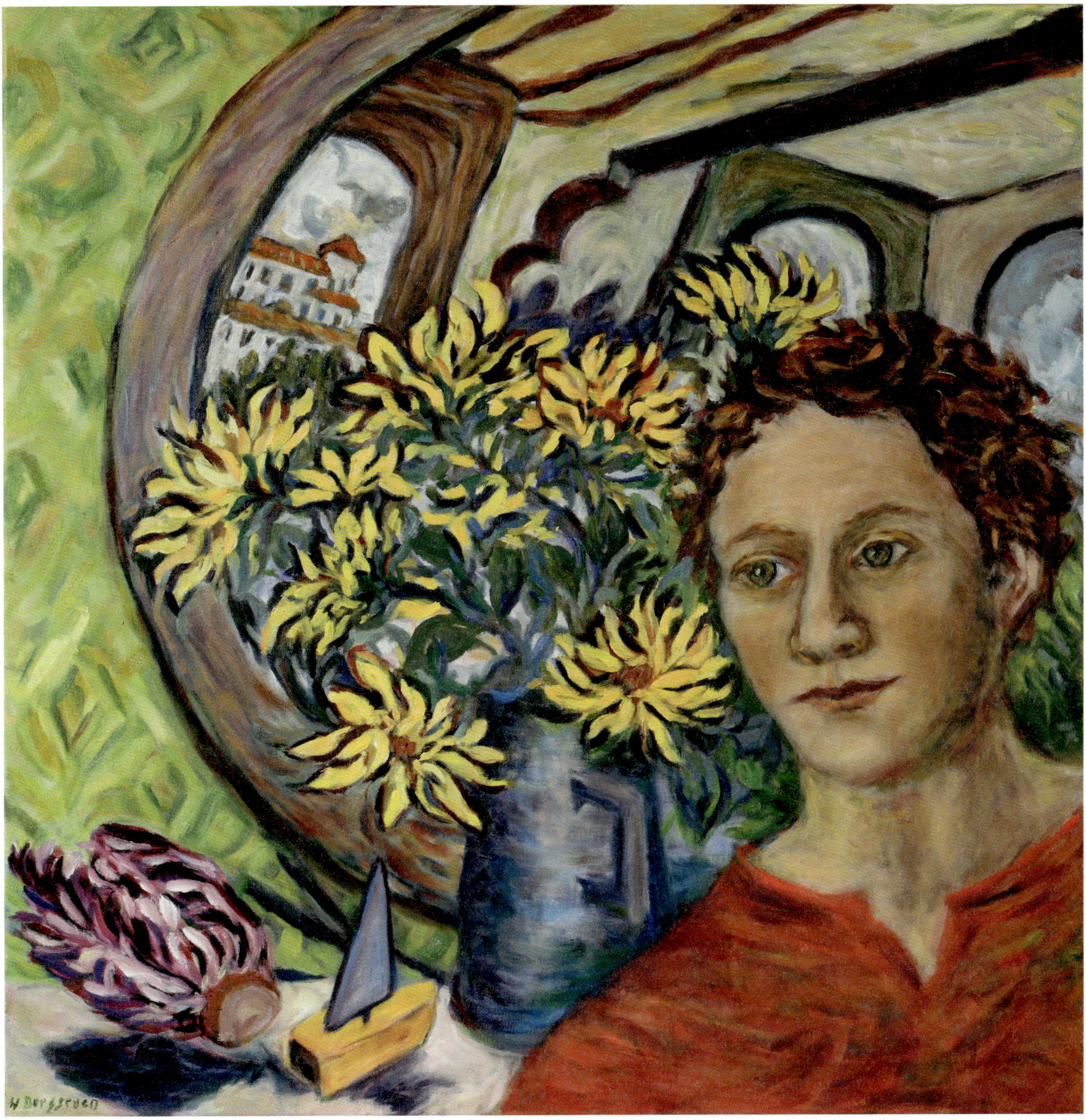

L'Assemblée Nationale, 1995–2025
Oil on canvas
105.4 × 80 cm
41½ × 31½ in

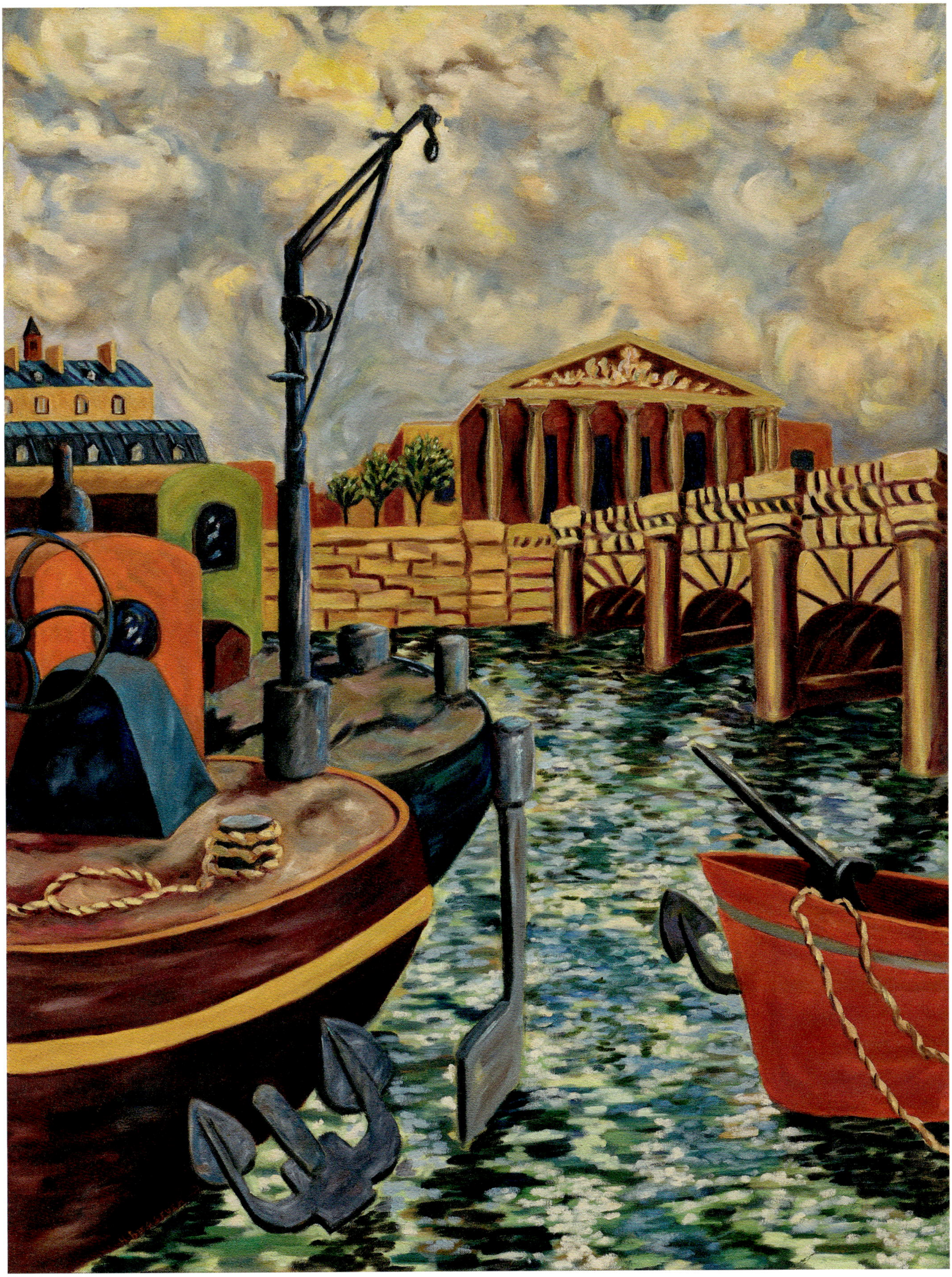

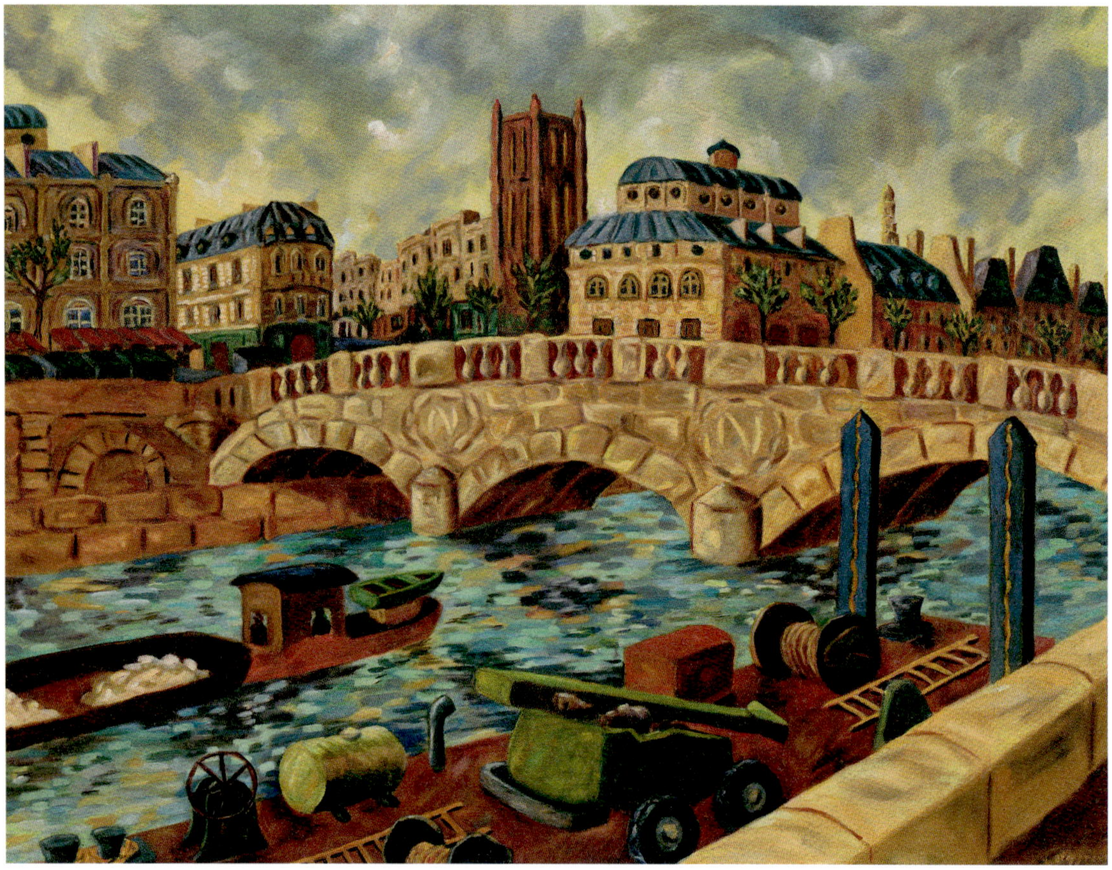

Pont au Change, 1995–2025
Oil on canvas
80 × 105.4 cm
31½ × 41½ in

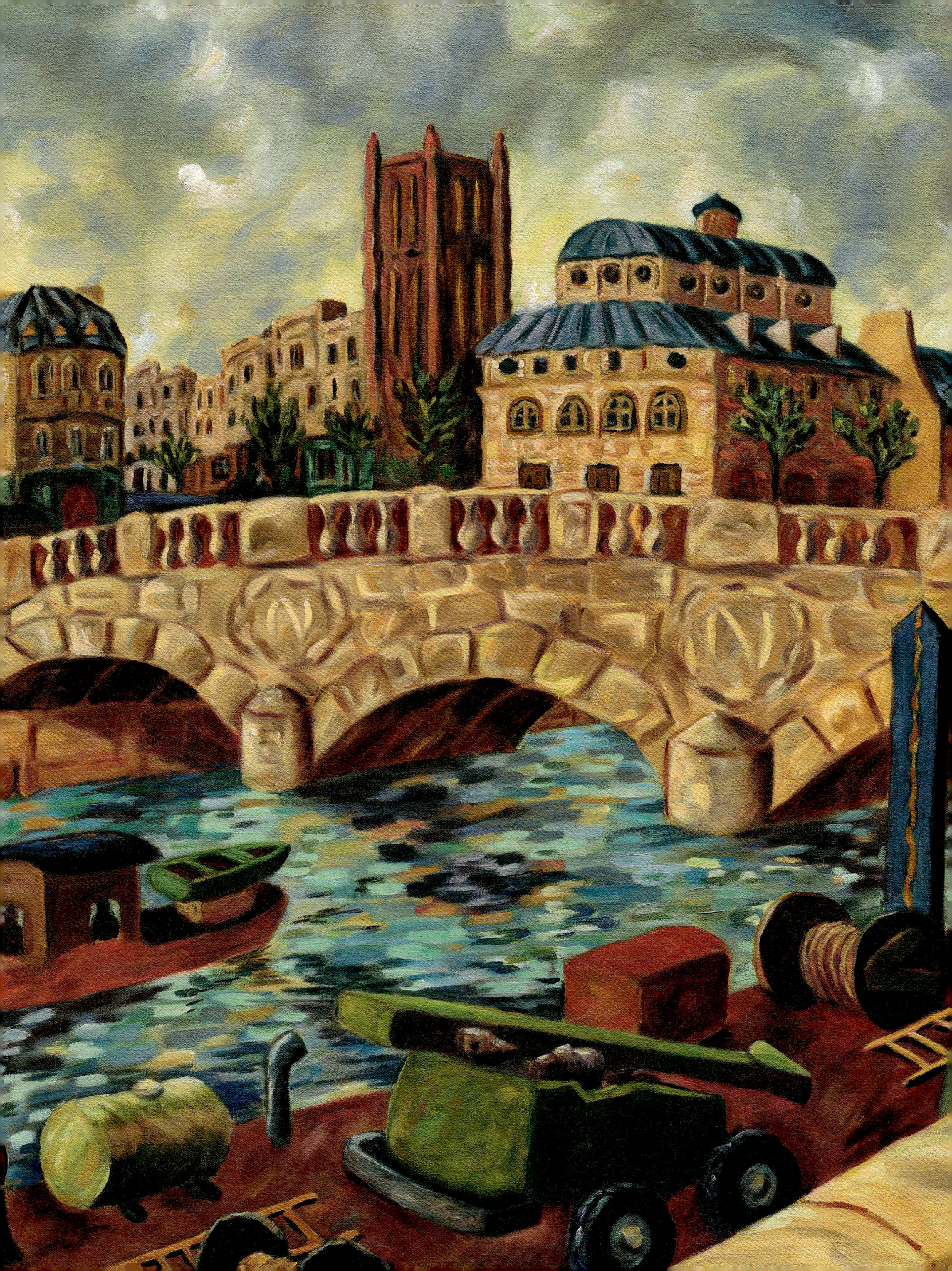

Passerelle, 1995–2013
Oil on canvas
91.4 × 121.9 cm
36 × 48 in

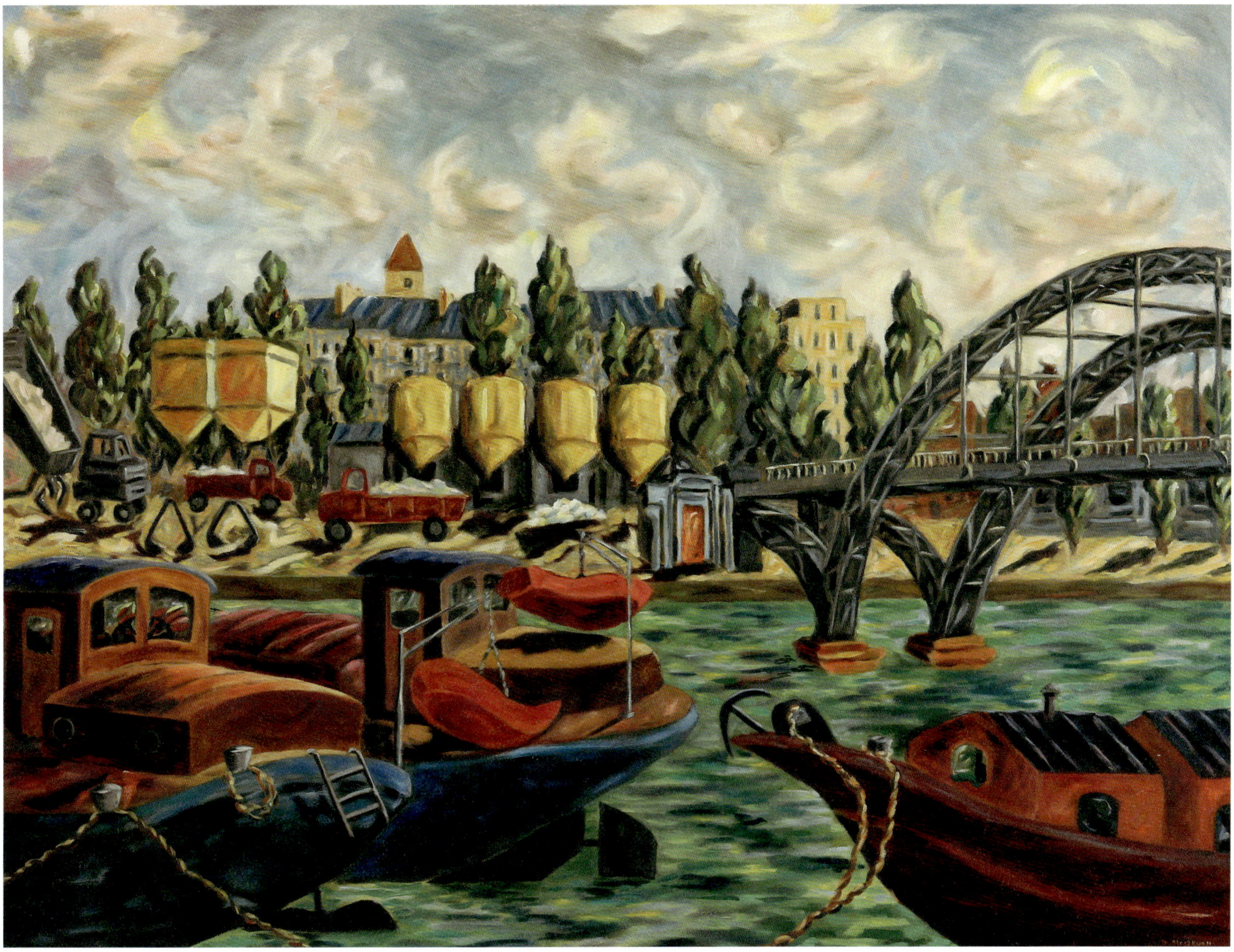

Map Maker, 2023
Oil on linen
101.6 × 76.2 cm
40 × 30 in

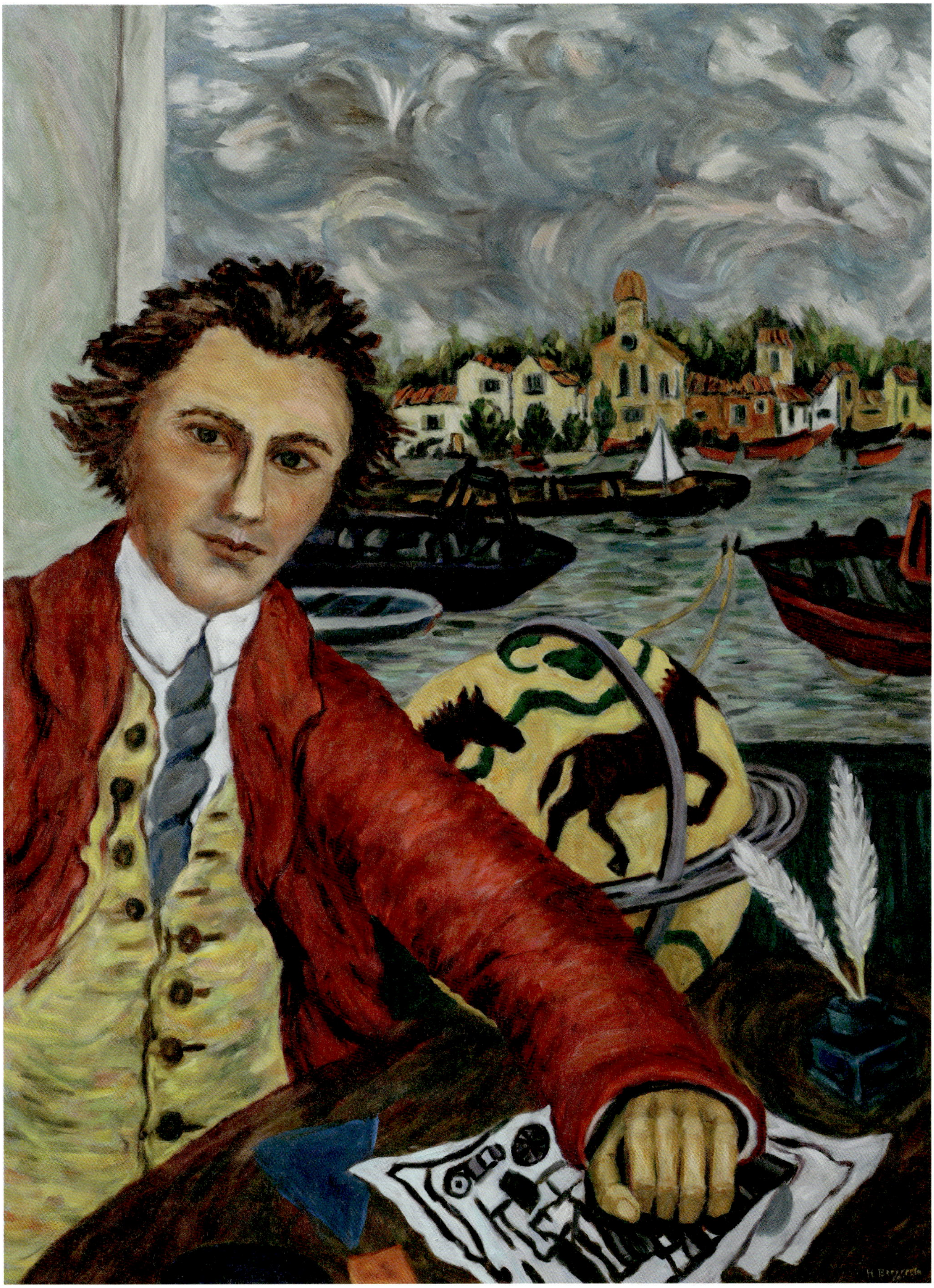

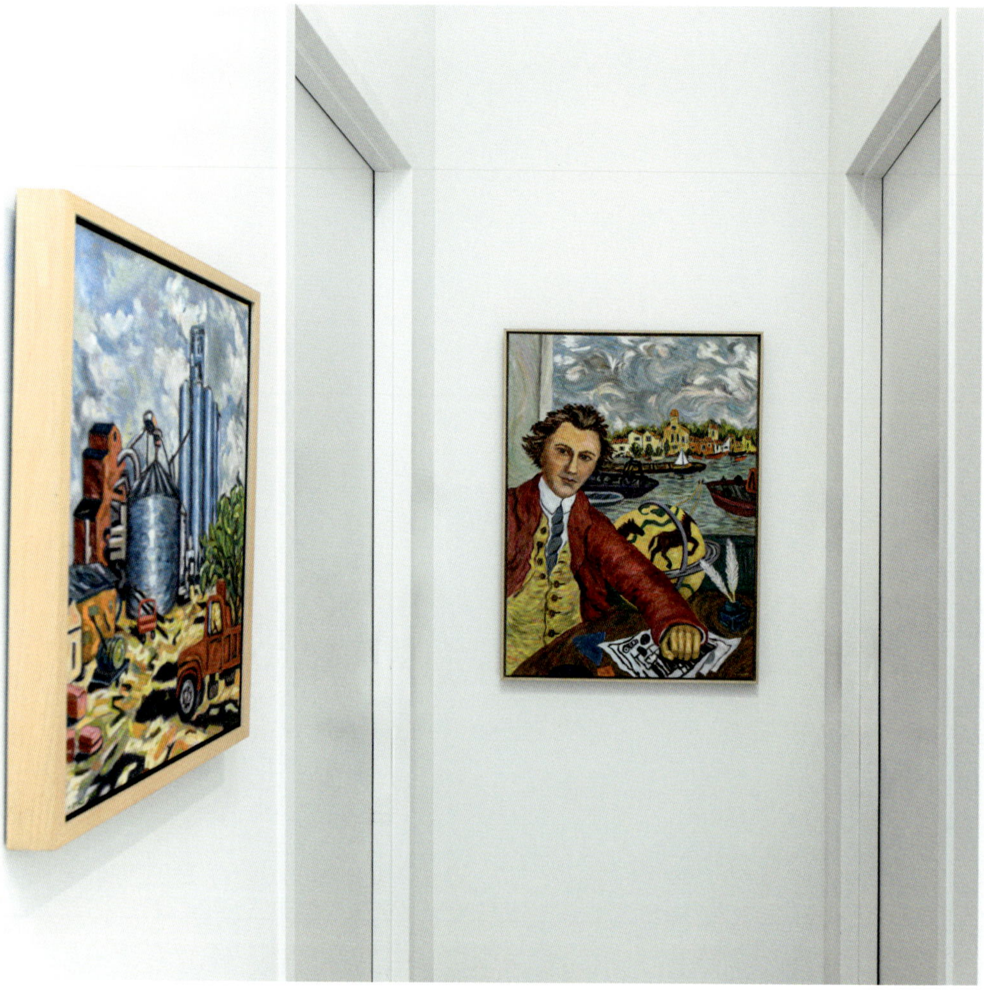

Exhibition views of *Helen Berggruen*
Berggruen Gallery, San Francisco
26 June – 14 August 2025

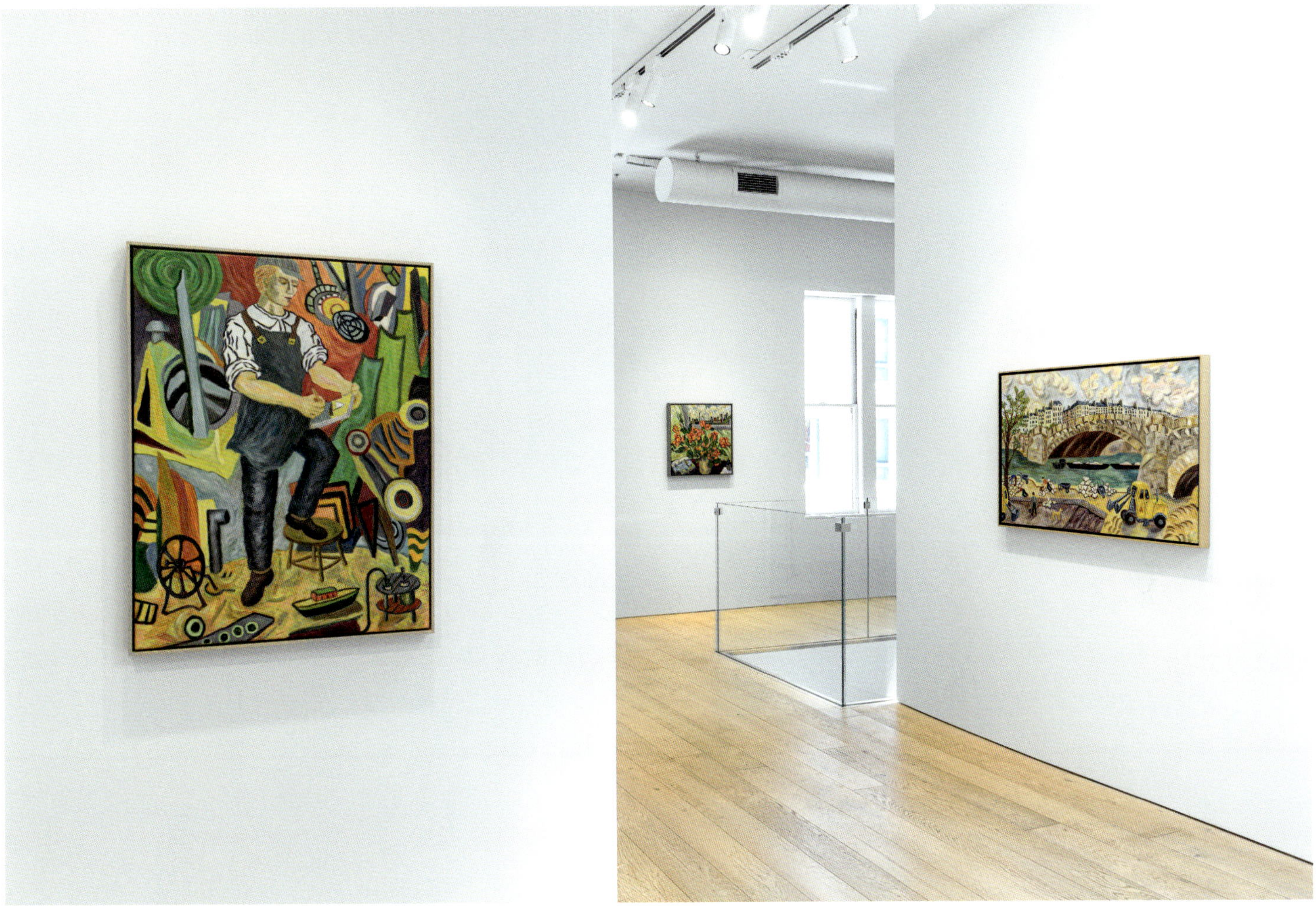

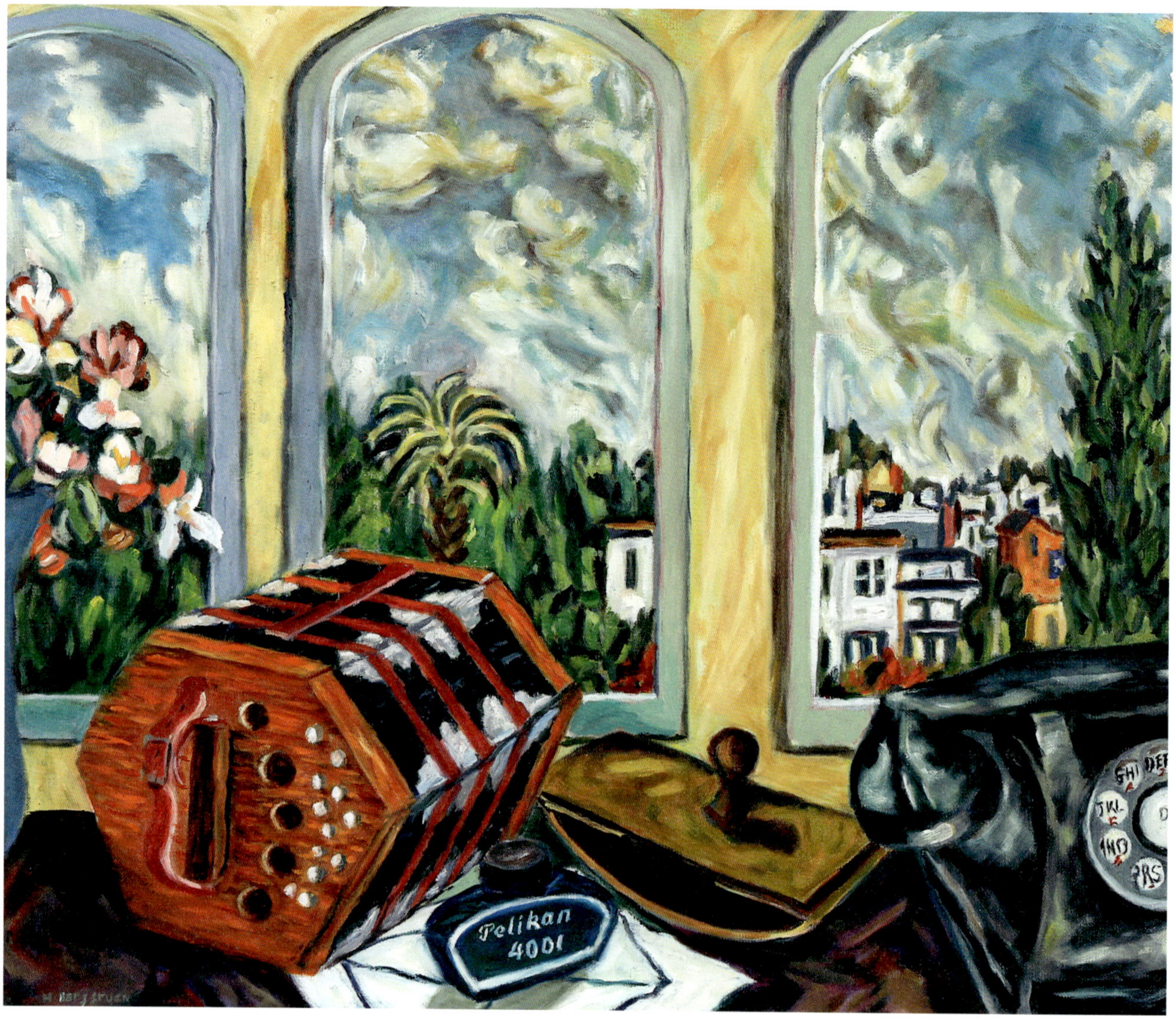

Ink, Concertina and Telephone, 2013–15
Oil on linen
45.7 × 61 cm
18 × 24 in

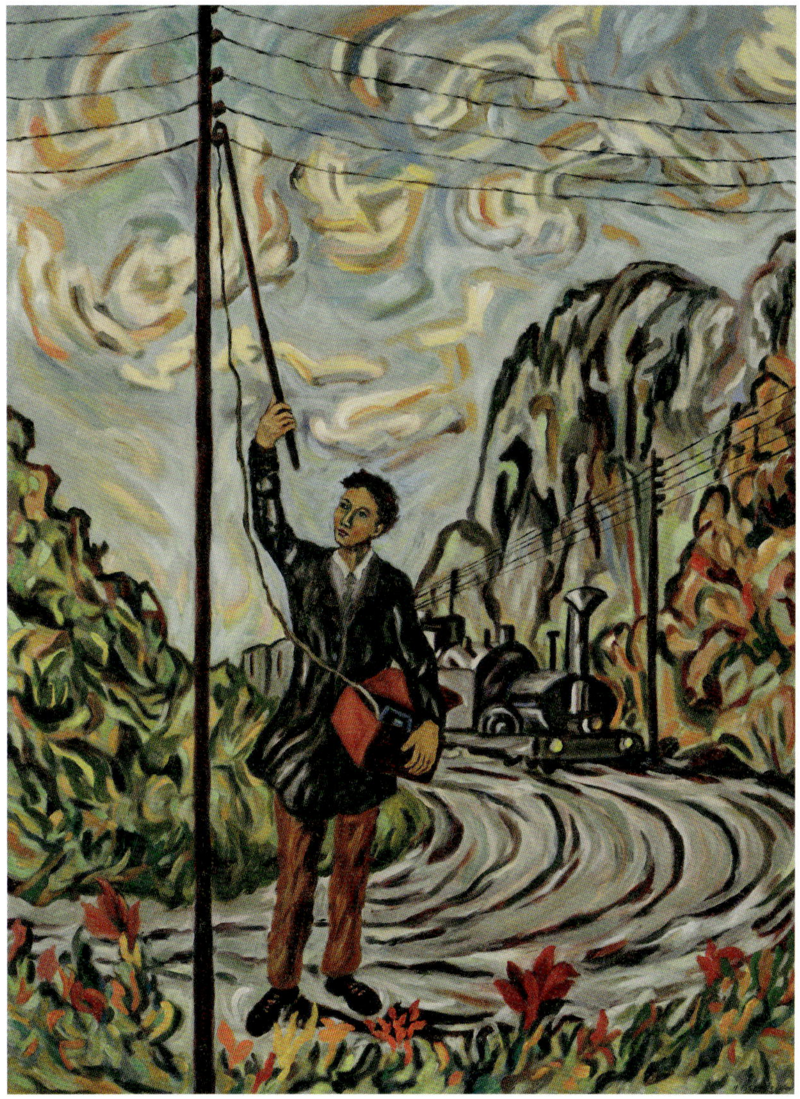

Junction Signal, Western Pass, 2024
Oil on linen
101.6 × 76.2 cm
40 × 30 in

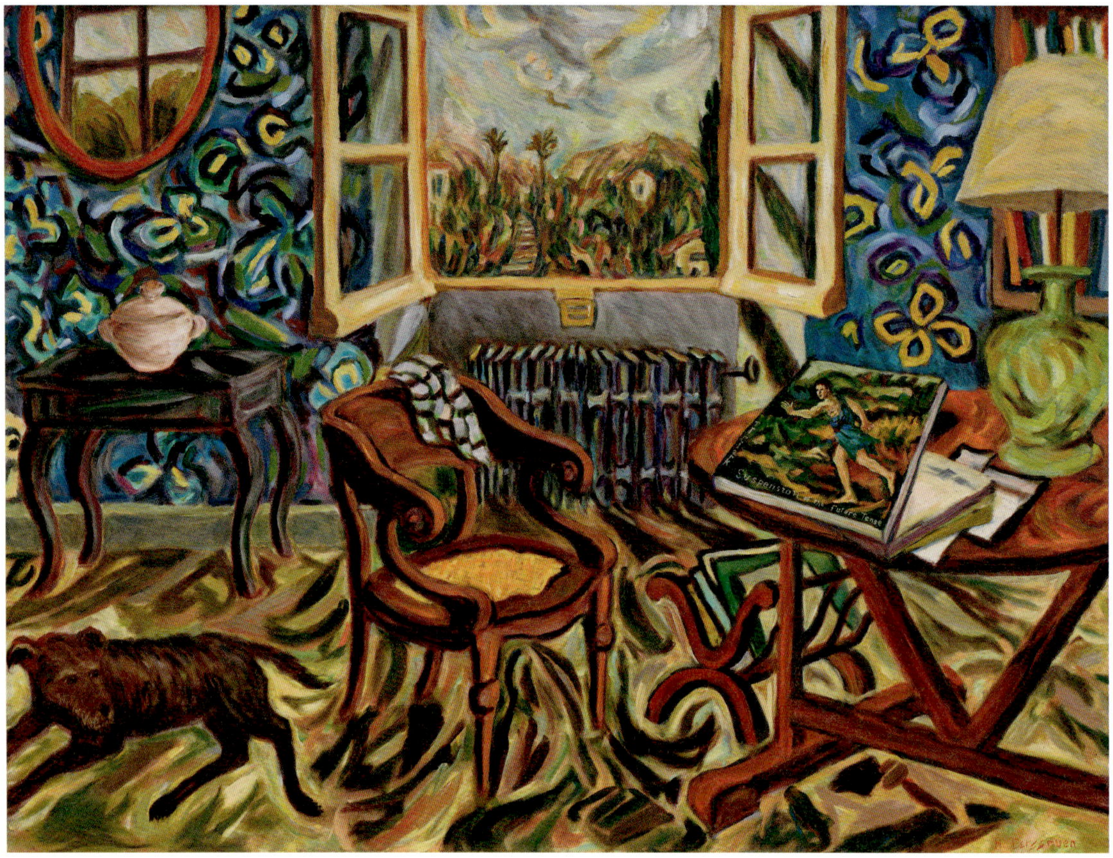

Suspension of the Future Tense, 2025
Oil on linen
76.2 × 101.6 cm
30 × 40 in

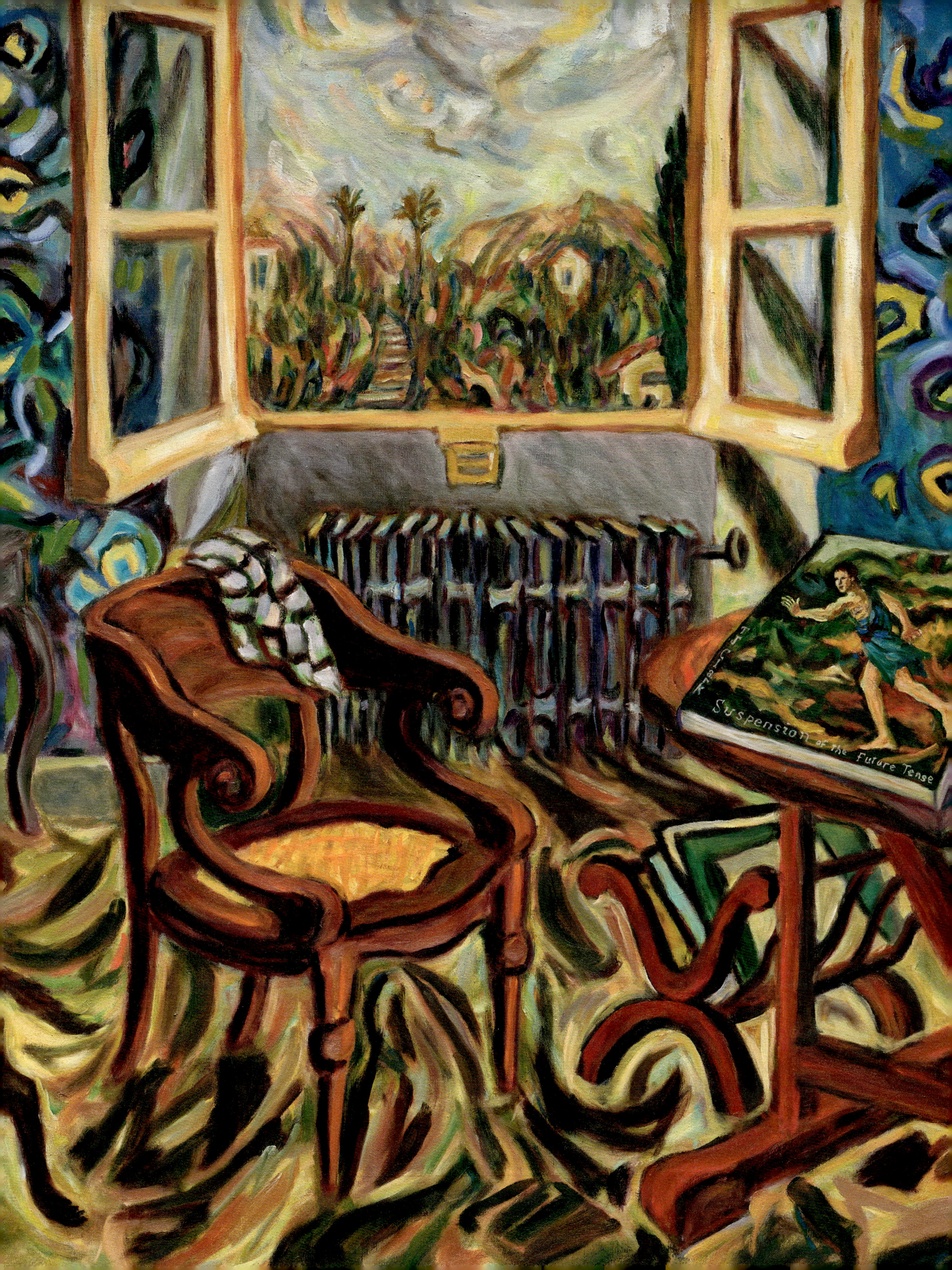
T J Clark
Suspension of the Future Tense

Wait for Dial Tone, 2024
Oil on canvas
101.6 × 76.2 cm
40 × 30 in

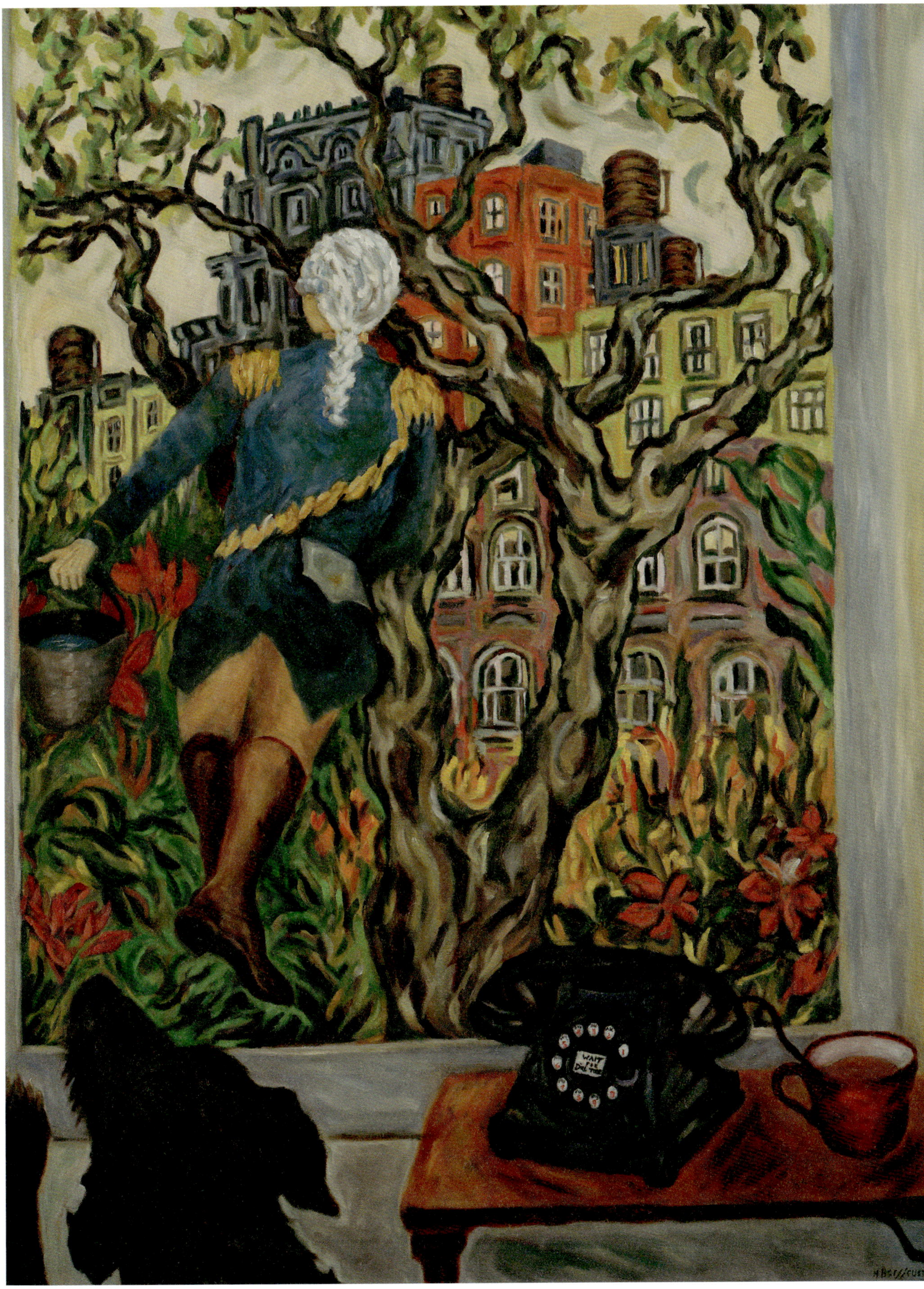
WAIT

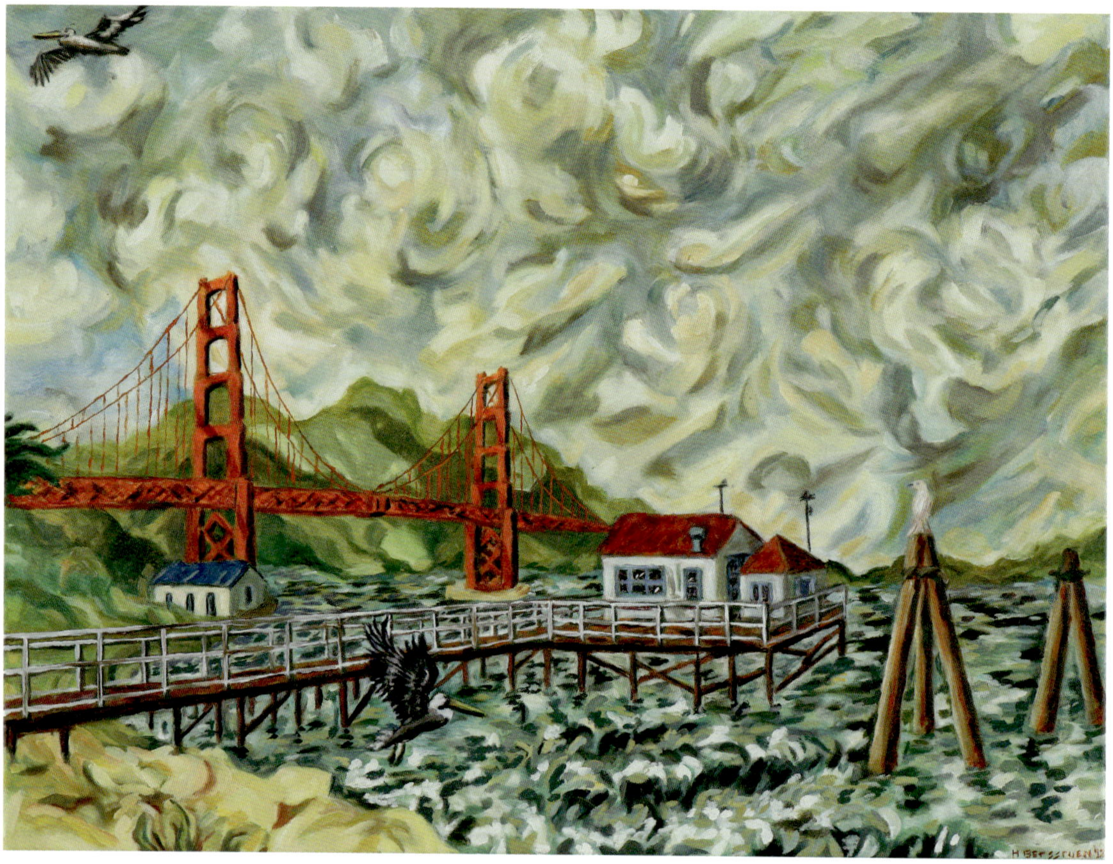

Golden Gate Bridge from Crissy Field, 2012
Oil on linen
45.7 × 61 cm
18 × 24 in

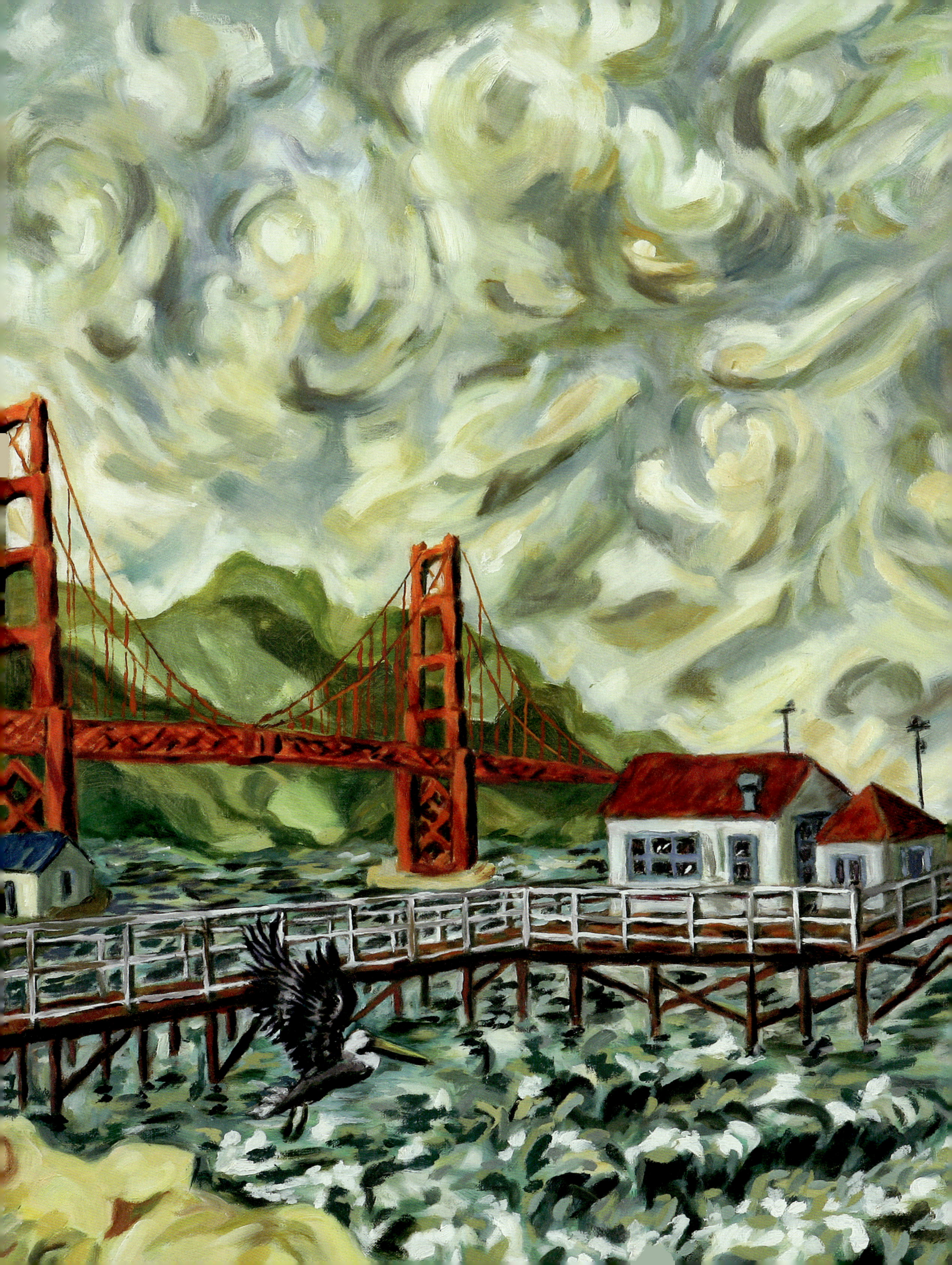

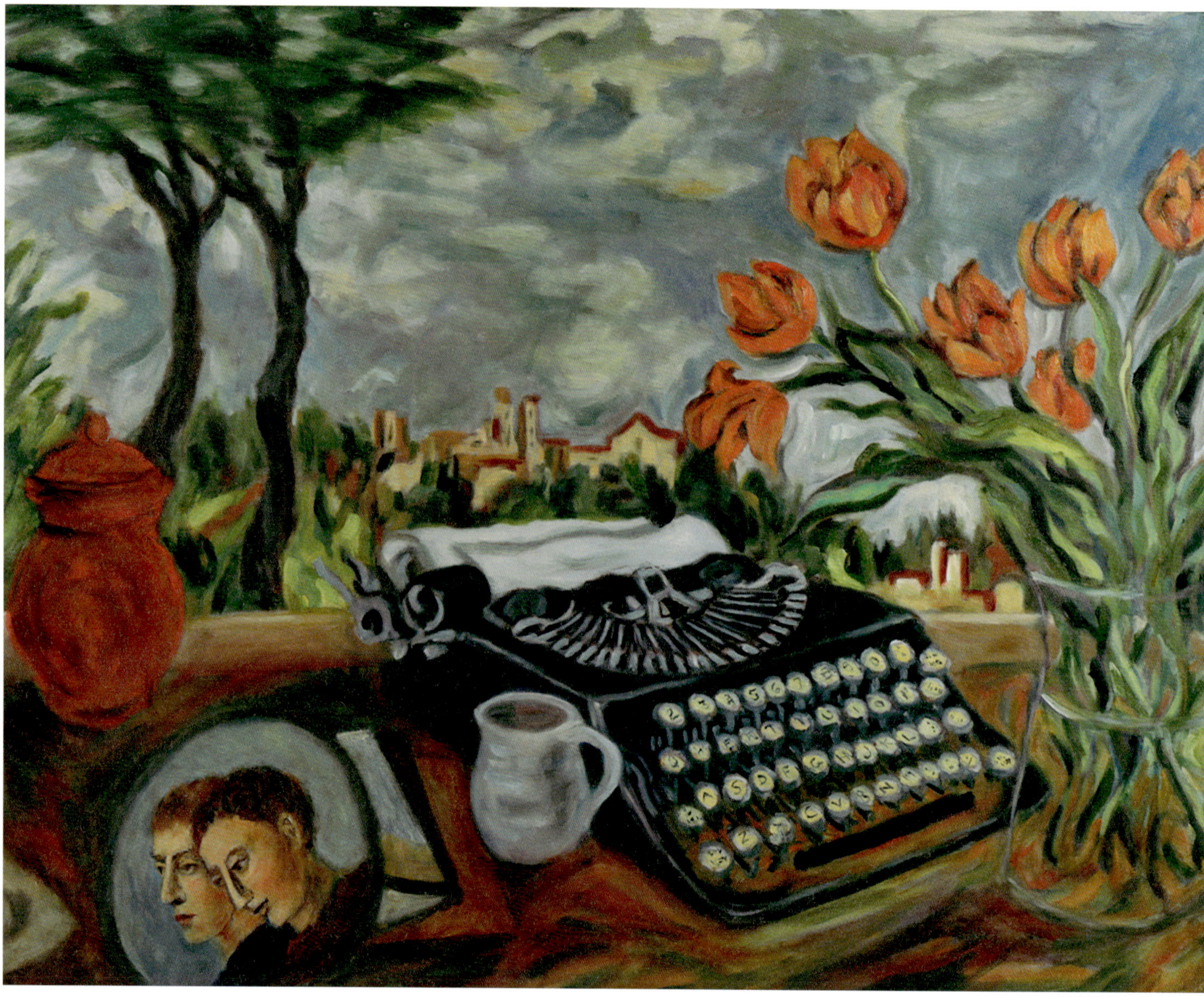

Between Two Worlds, 2018
Oil on linen
55.9 × 71.1 cm
22 × 28 in

Artist Interview
Jeff Gunderson in Conversation with Helen Berggruen

It's a pleasure seeing these paintings with you [at Berggruen Gallery].

One of the many intriguing things about your work is how much is enmeshed in each painting, and then you look at all of them and you realise there's much more. Emily McVarish wrote that some of the paintings are like windows onto far-flung landscapes and that's true for a lot of them. In fact, we're standing next to one of them – *The Message* [2022] – a beautiful painting which has a landscape and yet it's an interior as well.

This is a good one to start with, because it contains ingredients featured in many of my interiors, such as objects of communication that are no longer used, like typewriters and ink blotters. Hilary, my partner, has a wonderful collection of typewriters; they clamoured to make their appearance in at least one or two paintings. In *The Message* there's a typewriter and paper with something being written, but it's not clear what. Also, outside the window, I wanted there to be an imaginary landscape. In conceiving the structure of the painting, I decided the weight would be nearly evenly distributed between exterior and interior. The trees and buildings would be derived from Renaissance visions. Then I thought, 'While we're at it, let's bring some birds into the situation.' This painting passed through different phases. For a while there were two birds, but later I decided that there needed to be a third, flying with great determination towards the typewriter, and that it possibly could be delivering a message. Another factor in this picture that shows up in other interiors and still lifes is a sense of the present moment. A half-empty cup of coffee on the table indicates that somebody just left the room a moment ago.

Even though there are not always figures in your paintings, there seem to have been figures in the painting right beforehand – as you explain here, a cup of coffee that's half-drunk. Do you feel the sense of stillness, and yet that animated aspect occupying the pictorial space?

It's not necessarily my intention, though you and others have commented on this aspect of simultaneous stillness and movement. I think that goes along with the oppositions that are present in a lot of the paintings, or perhaps more accurately complements, like past/present, interior/exterior, abstract/representational, real/imagined. The coffee cup is the present, that's for sure, and the bird flying in. Although in a way this bird could be in somebody's imagination. The landscape is imagined; the birds could be too.

Let's move to a painting which has some of those same elements. It shows windows, in this case windows onto another 'far-flung landscape', yet has an interior that is intriguing.

We're now looking at *Le Salon de Mme Basseraux* [2001-25]. First, I should say that almost every work in this exhibition began with a 2B pencil and a sketchbook. The sketches were done on-site, and then eventually each drawing was transferred from paper to canvas and painted in the studio, in most cases far away from the original triggering subject. Only one piece in the whole show was inspired by a photograph, which I'll tell you about later. The sketch for *Le Salon de Mme Basseraux* was made in the south-west of France, where I have spent a lot of time over the course of the last two decades.

Mme Basseraux has lived in this house for many, many years. One day she invited me to come in and draw with my pencils. This isn't a still life with a far-flung landscape, it is an interior filled with Mme Basseraux's wonderful furniture. I may have exaggerated the curves and lines of the chairs, but the originals are definitely from another, more ornate time. She lives there now. The house dates from the mid-nineteenth century. Mme B's writing desk is featured in the painting; we see that someone has been writing something at the desk. There are books on the shelves. I love books. They show up in any interior whenever possible. Outside the window is a rather abstract version of the actual village. For me, the landscape outside a window is an opportunity for abstraction, whereas inside, I'm trying to represent somewhat more realistic qualities of the furniture and objects.

Different as this painting is from *The Message,* there are themes that are the same. The communication theme is certainly there; no typewriter, but there's the writing desk, and obviously it's used for communicating.

Yes, and as we look at the faded photographs and mementos on the mantel, we can imagine lives from the past connected to those who live in the space in the present.

I love that there's a painting within this painting. I was wondering if you could talk about that; or is it just purely extraneous?

I think I added it. I'm not sure what it was; that was also an opportunity for something rather abstract, and for more colour. There's a lot of pink and green in this painting, and orange, and I thought, 'Let's just add this painting hanging here.' It is interesting; I said I would talk about drawing later, but I'll bring it up now. I was in this room working on the drawing, which was just eight and a half by eleven inches, and the painting is forty-eight by sixty-four inches. It's big, but the drawing was small. A lot happens between a drawing and a painting. Often on the canvas I take the line drawing as a basis and completely invent the colours. In this case, the colours are influenced by the original palette in the house, because Mme Basseraux has chosen unusual colours in her nineteenth-century house – that's why we get all those pinks and greens.

I've looked at this painting for the past month and I continue to find new things. I see the piece that's in front of the fireplace, the screen that's absolutely fascinating, a totally different element of the painting – it can stand as a painting on its own, as an abstract, as you were saying.

Frequently, there is quite a time gap between the original drawing of any interior, and then what happens later in the studio. Using an overhead projector – very low tech, it has two bright light bulbs in it, and a little mirror – I project the drawing onto a canvas, render the drawing in charcoal on the canvas, and then eventually start blocking out colour. I recall that the fabric on this fireplace screen was a kind of cream colour with green stripes, though I'm not sure. It's true, I relish the idea of doing something abstract in the middle of an otherwise fairly defined representation of an interior, with table and chairs, a mantelpiece, curtains and windows.

Quiet as this painting is, somewhat a still life, there is so much going on – a cacophony of ideas, and thoughts, and movement in it at the same time. The concurrence is just enthralling.

And now... to a landscape; we will move outside.

This painting is called *L'Assemblée Nationale* [1995–2025]. This one is more – I was going to say seascape, although it's not a seascape; it's a water-and-bridge-and-barge-scape. There's not much land in it. It's divided between water and sky, with large barges filling a lot of the space, and a big sky. This is part of a series that I started in Paris some years ago, and I ended up working on them more lately, which is why they have a long time-span. In 1995 I was in Paris and became very intrigued seeing the different barges, trucks and working machinery, and their juxtaposition against the bridges and buildings that may be one, two, three or even four hundred years old.

We walked to this canvas because we wanted to talk about a landscape, but you're right, this is a maritime picture. There isn't any land! Although it's a cityscape too with a beautiful rendering of Paris. You can paint water! It's beautiful water, and water is very difficult for photographers or for painters, but this – for somebody who's in the water a lot, and in open water, as I am – is a really terrific water painting. And there's the sky, which is reflective of the water; the two go together so well in this painting. And then those contraptions of the barges, anchors, pulley, rope and all the other nautical elements.

It's the juxtaposition; the big anchor in the foreground and another anchor on the other side. I'm going to go back to the observation that, at least until recently, there were very few human figures in my work. As we saw in *The Message*, in the still lifes and interiors there's often a sense that somebody's just left the room or is about to come back. The landscapes are an example of how I worked when I first started painting. When I stopped working in theatre and turned to the solitary easel, I decided that my paintings would be like little stages. Instead of having humans on the stage, however, there would be objects communicating with each other and I would try to animate them. So from the earliest time of when I started painting, that was what I tried to do: the anchor, ropes, pulleys and all that, juxtaposed – in this case – against water and the ancient bridge of Paris and the Assemblée Nationale, and the skies. We'll talk about the skies more later.

It truly is a maritime painting within a city scene. I misspoke when I said 'rope'; these are 'lines', because they are part of ships and barges. There is a human presence and a human hand on everything in this image and yet, at the same time, a beautiful rendering of nature.

Let's look at another barge painting. This one's called *Passerelle* [1995–2013], which refers to the large bridge. As I walked around the streets of Paris, I was continually struck by the vitality of barges and working trucks and cranes. One day I found myself, armed with pencils and sketchbook, on a quay looking across the Seine, and what should I see? In the foreground, barges, some of which have become habitations, and some still transporting cargo. Behind the barges, I couldn't believe my luck! Silos, maintenance equipment and a dump truck loaded with mysterious white stuff, perhaps gravel. I set to work immediately. For these Parisian riverscapes, I discovered the best time to do the drawings was during the long Parisian lunch hour. Since it takes me about an hour and a half to accomplish a drawing, I would thus be undisturbed.

I think here I'll turn the spotlight onto one of the major influences on my painting – van Gogh. Although many elements, movements and artists have influenced my style and approach to painting, van Gogh is high on the list, for the astonishing energy – the ecstatic rhythm and force of his brushstrokes; the clashing, impossible violet and carmine shadows under olive trees... the wild and dramatic skies...

Among the principles that guided van Gogh and the Expressionists was a belief in the power of the artist to create a vision of the world as it ought to be. This idea captivates me. I've approached the barges plying the Seine and romanticised them. Those barges are working and behind them is an industrial scene. For some reason I'm very attracted to industrial elements in the urban setting, and especially in Paris. What city is more romantic than Paris? But then there are silos and tractors in the middle of it. Those stone bridges need to be maintained! Or there's a painting with a tractor in front of a store front [*Yellow Tractor, Paris Storefront*, 1994–2025] – a huge contrast between the vehicle and the Parisian façades. There are a lot of almost opposites in these paintings – things that don't quite belong there, but they're there.

This might be a good time to ask you about when you decided to leave theatre work, and that you were going to do carpentry – your construction work on a very famous San Francisco project.

Before moving away from the subject of theatre, I would like to pay a tribute to someone who profoundly influenced my life and the direction it took: Robert Wilson, the great opera and theatre director, who died on 31 July [2025].

I was fortunate enough to perform with Robert Wilson's theatre troupe in the early 1970s in Europe and New York. It was thrilling and powerful to be among that band of players. As a director, Bob sustained an atmosphere that was at once demanding and marvellously expansive. Bob invited and encouraged each of us to bring to specific situations more of ourselves than we realised we were capable of, to bring our own creativity to the whole, to make it greater than the sum of its parts. All of us felt inspired and lucky to be part of a unique moment of American theatre and dance.

Even though a long while passed before I began to devote myself in earnest to being a painter, I believe that the inspiration of working on pieces such as *Deafman Glance* [1971], the invitation to add our voices to Bob's powerful vision, to enter a state of opened imagination, all had a huge impact. Creating on stage a special atmosphere filled with beauty and visual images, as well as a complex sound world, influenced my decision to become a painter and affected what eventually happened on the canvas. One element that I believe has transferred over from that long-ago experience in theatre is that in the action of painting, I remain conscious of the possibility of a special communication between stage and audience, or in this case, between canvas and viewer. I heartily express my gratitude to Bob. His legacy will endure.

After I stopped working with Bob, a group of us launched a small theatre company, producing experimental projects throughout the streets of New York. At a certain point in the late 1970s, longing to be near the Pacific Ocean, I came back to San Francisco, determined to learn a practical skill. I applied, and was accepted, as an apprentice carpenter, becoming a card-carrying member of the local union. At that time – the time of affirmative action – whenever a construction company received a federal government building contract, the company was obliged to hire a certain number of women and a certain number of minorities, and so they hired me! And I worked on – yes – the Moscone Center. What would become a huge convention centre was just a giant hole in the ground at the time! The foreman assigned some very monotonous work to me. Part of the job entailed attending apprentice school at night to learn the laws regarding building codes and things like that. Being part of a large construction crew was a really interesting experience. I rode the bus to the job site every day, carrying my lunch pail and my hard hat. However, I soon found that I was far from being a natural at construction; I did not grow up with a hammer in my hand, and after a few months I left. But afterwards I did work on other construction projects; I learned a lot more about carpentry and was able to fix up the place where I was living, and that's when I started painting. I built myself a tiny studio.

I think that first-person experience with carpentry – with anything that one does in life – can be so evident in one's artwork, and it sure is with yours. There's a great respect for tools in all of the paintings. This is not the only painting that shows construction work. Plenty of your paintings show tools and the reverence for things that are handmade and manufactured in big settings like this. It's very evident that you come to it with some real knowledge.

That's interesting. I have to say, I think it would be improper to continue this interview without mentioning my father. This may seem like an odd moment to mention him, but he was an acclaimed art dealer and collector in Paris for many years after the war. I grew up in California. We were in touch over the years, and had a cordial relationship and wrote letters, but when he heard that I was trying to be a carpenter, he was emphatically *not* enthusiastic. However, soon after that, when I started painting, he was *very* enthusiastic. I had been hesitant to tell him I'd started painting, fearing that as a great connoisseur, he might be dismissive. But he wasn't at all! Papa told me my early watercolours reminded him of Matisse; that gave me a burst of confidence! My father surrounded himself with many different styles of modern art. Tristan Tzara and Max Ernst would play chess at his gallery. Dadaists and Surrealists and Modernists passed through his gallery. Yet, when he saw my paintings of tractors and cement mixers, he asked, puzzled, 'Why would anybody want to look at a tractor?' What could I say in reply? I was both speechless and at the same time more determined than ever, as I prepared an exhibition entitled *Machines et Véhicules à Paris* for the Alliance Française in San Francisco, and later for Fischbach Gallery in New York.

I think your father knew that your paintings were important.

How about another interior with a landscape...

The title of this painting is *Interior with Matadors* [2018]. The initial drawing for this was made – since we were just talking about my father – in his apartment, where he and his wife Bettina and their kids, my half-brothers Nicolas and Olivier, lived; they grew up there. Over the years, I spent a lot of time in that apartment and in that room. The furniture – the chair, the desk, the objects – all have a history, all are crafted beautifully. The dynamic patterns in the carpet found a central place in my initial drawing. Later, in the studio, over the course of months, the essential memory of that carpet became a jumping-off point to explore textures and patterns on the canvas through brushstrokes, marks and colours. And let's take the lamp; there's something special about the lamp. To me it's like a flying saucer; as though it had flown in from somewhere else. Of course, in fact, somebody made this lamp, and it's an extraordinary shape. The view outside is based on the Jardin du Luxembourg, with the Panthéon in the background; it's my version of that setting, and there are these amazing big glass doors that give one lots of opportunity to be able to put a landscape out there. I added a few books on the desk. For example, because of my passion for opera, I decided to place a classic work, Joseph Kerman's *Opera as Drama* [1956], on the desk.

... And the matadors on that beautiful wall that you include...

My father did have a collection of early modernist paintings and prints and drawings, especially Picasso; this lithograph or drawing of Picasso's matadors and bulls hung on the wall of the room. The wall was covered in striped fabric. Later, in the studio, this idea of that striped textile gave me something to dig into. As with Madame Basseraux's living room, there was existing colour on the walls, much more subtle in the actual apartment, but I exercised the licence to take it to a heightened, even exaggerated level on the canvas.

The abstract nature of these beautiful walls, as abstract painting, and then the books of course; as a librarian I sure do admire all the books that are in your paintings. This is one of the paintings that when I first saw it

intrigued me immensely, and still does, and I'm probably going to find ten more things within it that are fascinating – *Mantel with Globe & Telescope* [2013–2025].

The title says it all! You've got your home scene, you've got your wanderlust – your desire to wander; a globe is a wonderful object. You can spin it, you can imagine where you're going, where you might go. And the telescope is from the era when people travelled by sailing ships. Something might be out there on the rolling seas that you need to pay attention to. The globe and telescope are both symbols of possibility, of imagination. And the mantel was an excuse to make as many little brushstrokes as possible. This painting depicts rooms opening upon rooms, a spatial sense of more possibility beyond.

The intrigue of the mirror reflecting the rest of the room, and then another window, more books and the clock. It's a painting within a painting that's absorbing to someone like me, who's lost within what seems to be a small space, almost claustrophobic to begin with, and then you realise that it's not at all. It opens up to all the windows and other dimensions.

That's interesting. And then there's the actual outside, which is a real San Francisco back yard, not fanciful. And on the shelf is a little sailboat.

Again, the adventurer... I was thrilled to see *Map Maker* [2023], and the fact that it's such a *figurative* painting, a portrait.

This painting started out four years before, as a line drawing, as the barest of bare-bones sketches, which I did one day in 2019 when I found myself at the National Portrait Gallery in London, in front of a portrait of Sir Joseph Banks by Joshua Reynolds. I couldn't tear myself away from this portrait, and the most effective way to get inside it was to take out my pencils and see what happened. Well, the drawing turned out to be just a hint of what the Reynolds portrait portrayed. The drawing depicts a pensive young man with a slight smile, behind him the hint of a globe with no geography or anything on its surface, and in the upper right quarter of the sketch is a window frame, with nothing outside. So my sketch provided just a rough framework from which to develop a new figure in a new setting. With the intention of emphasising the globe, I remembered some photographs I'd taken a few years earlier, of Renaissance globes, in the Austrian National Library in Vienna.

Yes! I've been to that library! It's beautiful.

For my portrait of the map maker, since he was more or less a figure of the eighteenth century, I decided there should be quills on the table. Our cartographer would be engaged with some mysterious graphs. The globe would have horses trotting around it, rather than geographical locations. Outside the window is a backdrop derived from another drawing done during my earlier travels in Italy. The maritime buildings probably date back to the Middle Ages. I was able to surround my map maker with different eras and places. The centuries-old houses in the port town still exist; the boats in the harbour could be from any era. The view outside offers a window into another time, somewhere between real and imagined.

It's timeless. The harbour outside the window is almost like a painting within the painting; there are barges and seascape, and the beautiful, wonderful portrait with the intensity of this person, with his head of hair! Very painterly too, as all your paintings are, but it's fun to see them up close and see all the brushstrokes.

We'll look at one more figurative painting. I'll let you talk about the title and the composition.

The title is *Schoolboy with Satchel* [2025]. Every painting in this exhibition, every single one of them, began on site with either a pencil drawing or an oil sketch, except for this one. This is the only painting that was derived from a photograph; the photograph in question is a small sepia portrait dated 1920 on the back, taken in a Berlin portrait studio. The subject of this portrait is my father at six years old. He probably arrived for the session carrying his satchel, but I bet you they gave him that big cone with something like candy in it to hold in his arms. The photograph is very poignant; Papa's expression is rather wistful. I decided to do what I could to situate him well on the canvas and give him some of the same qualities as in the photograph. Then I wondered where exactly to locate him. Certainly not in the photographer's studio! And so, looking back at some drawings and some paintings from my time in the south-west of France, I surrounded the young Heinz with hay rolls and fields, as a backdrop on his way home from school.

And the most abstracted sky of all your paintings that are here.

It's pretty abstract.

But again, that animation, that landscape, that sense of movement and yet stillness; the boy stands as if being photographed, ready to head off into the world.

Somebody at the opening said to me, 'There are no shadows in your paintings!' I said, 'Oh really?'

[Laughter]

I think that shows you have a real command of light!

Ha! Yes, that's right!

This has been terrific, Helen. Thank you very much!

Thank you!

Let's do it again tomorrow!

***Passerelle*, 1995–2013**
(detail)
Oil on canvas
91.4 × 121.9 cm
36 × 48 in

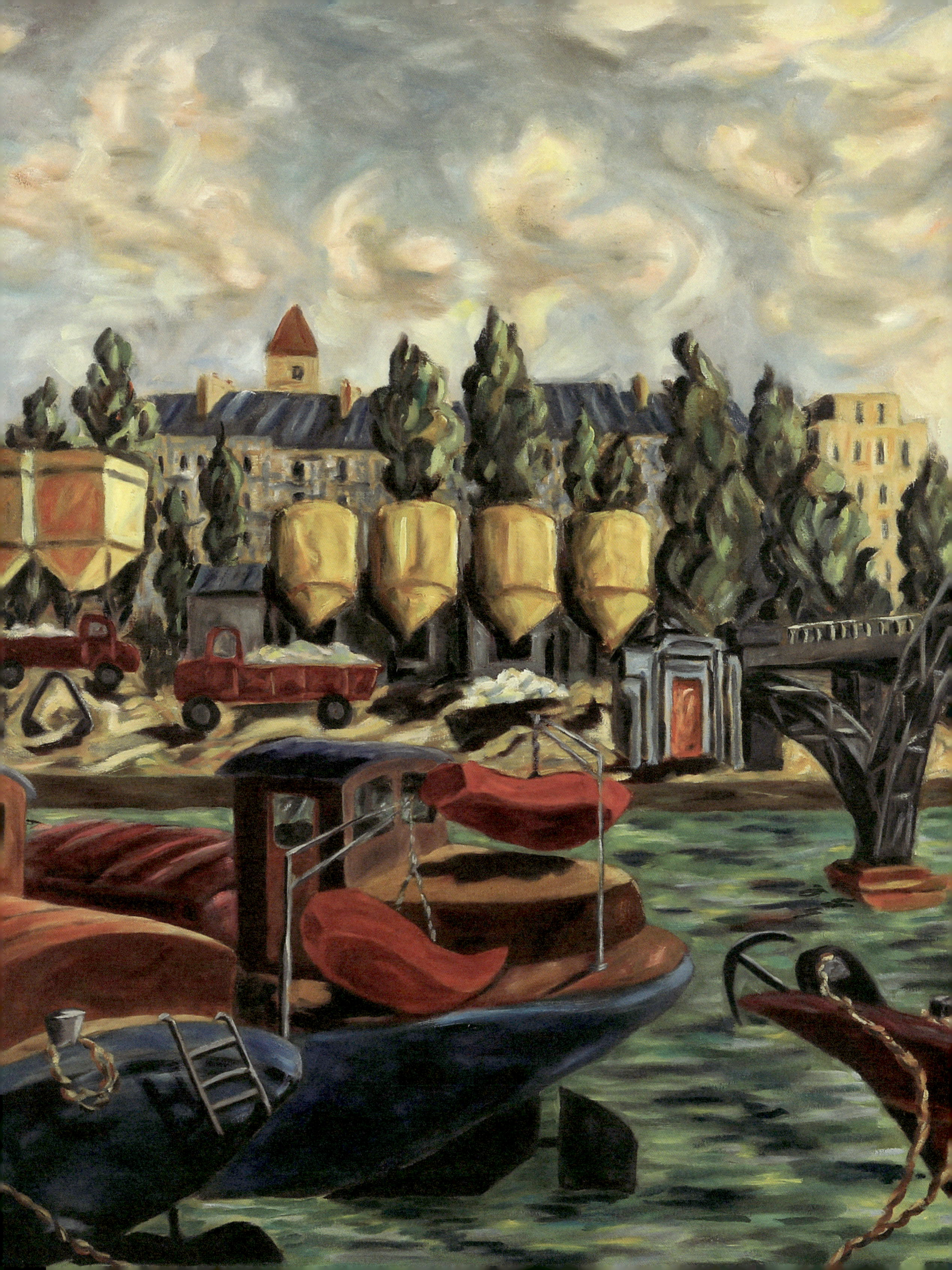

Artist Biography

After an early career working in experimental theatre with such internationally acclaimed directors as Robert Wilson and Peter Schumann, in the early 1980s Helen Berggruen stepped away from communal stage life towards a more solitary focus in the painting studio. Primary influences include Persian and Indian miniatures, Dutch seventeenth-century painters, Mantegna, Constable, van Gogh, the post-Impressionists, French Fauvism and German Expressionism. Based in San Francisco, Berggruen's work has been exhibited and collected throughout Iowa, at The Demuth Museum in Lancaster, Pennsylvania, and in London, Berlin, south-west France, New York and San Francisco.

Contributors

Craig Burnett

Craig Burnett's books include *The Lost Works of Johan Riding* (Mörel), *Philip Guston: The Studio* (Afterall) and *Jeff Wall* (Tate). He has written widely about art, including essays and articles on Lucas Arruda, John Ashbery, Luca Bertolo, Gregory Crewdson, Stan Douglas, Geoffrey Farmer, Hugo van der Goes, Rodney Graham, Emma Hart, Utagawa Hiroshige, Rachel Howard, Shara Hughes, Nicolas Poussin, Dana Schutz, Erin Shirreff, John Stezaker, Luc Tuymans and Stephen Waddell, among others. He lives in London.

Jeff Gunderson

Jeff Gunderson, an archivist with the San Francisco Art Institute Legacy Foundation & Archive, was previously the long-time librarian with SFAI. He has written on the history of Californian art and photography, as well as essays on the sculptor Adaline Kent and tattoo artist Ed Hardy, and he wrote the introductory essay to *Black Power/Flower Power: Photographs by Pirkle Jones and Ruth-Marion Baruch.* Gunderson has given presentations on artists Joan Brown, Elmer Bischoff, Ed Ruscha and Carlos Villa; the history of San Francisco conceptual art; and the influence of art libraries on artists. He is currently working on a collection of essays about open-water swimming.

Mary Kate Tankard

Mary Kate Tankard is a writer working in public relations and communications at Berggruen Gallery in San Francisco. She has curated group exhibitions and written for local and national publications. She was the Profile Editor for GLOBUS and a literary organiser for the Global Women's Rights Forum at the University of San Francisco. For Berggruen's editorial section she conducts artist interviews, writes exhibition text and produces video content. Before joining Berggruen Gallery, she worked at the San Francisco International Film Festival.

Helen Berggruen
The Song Inside of Things

Published by Hurtwood Press Limited, London
Part of the *Hurtwood Artist & Gallery Series*

Series editor: Anneka French
Series design: Alice Daisy Pomfret

Project editor: Anneka French
Proofreading: William Lambie
Layout design: Alice Daisy Pomfret
Reprography and production: Hurtwood Press

Each publication in the *Hurtwood Artist & Gallery Series* presents new, recent and selected works by a single artist working nationally and internationally today. Along with a foreword by an established art world professional, the series features specially commissioned essays and interviews with the artist by leading writers, art historians and curators, offering in-depth insight. Central to each publication are the exhibitions and galleries that help to spotlight some of the most engaging artists of today.

Artist acknowledgements:
I would like to acknowledge my brother, John Berggruen, for inviting me to exhibit my work at his gallery in 2025. The entire staff at Berggruen Gallery was incredibly communicative and helpful. Many thanks to Friedhelm Krey, whose essay for a 2013 catalogue of my work at Fischbach Gallery inspired the title of this book. The title of Friedhelm's essay was 'The Song Inside All Things'. That title was an allusion to a proverbial line of poetry, 'A song is sleeping in all things', by the acclaimed German Romantic poet Joseph von Eichendorff. I'd like to express gratitude to my partner Hilary Rand, for her patience, useful suggestions and encouragement throughout the project.

Thank you to Craig Burnett, Jeff Gunderson and Mary Kate Tankard for their insightful written contributions to this publication and to talented photographers Don Felter, Shaun Roberts and Izzi Valencia. Thanks also to the team at Hurtwood: Francis Atterbury, Anneka French, Louise Frith, Joanna Hilton, Roger Jones, Seb Lansdowne and Matt Price; to designer Alice Daisy Pomfret; and proofreader William Lambie.

Published in 2026 by Hurtwood Press Limited, London

ISBN: 978-0-903696-99-9

Printed and bound in the UK by Gomer using FSC Mix

MIX
Paper | Supporting responsible forestry
FSC® C114687
FSC www.fsc.org

A catalogue record for this book is available from the British Library.

Cover image: *The Message*, 2022, (detail)